TRUST
ME

TRUST ME

FOUR STEPS to AUTHENTICITY and CHARISMA

NICK MORGAN

JOSSEY-BASS
A Wiley Imprint
www.josseybass.com

Published by Jossey-Bass
A Wiley Imprint
989 Market Street, San Francisco, CA 94103-1741—www.josseybass.com

Jossey-Bass books and products are available through most bookstores. To contact Jossey-Bass directly call our Customer Care Department within the U.S. at 800-956-7739, outside the U.S. at 317-572-3986, or fax 317-572-4002.

Jossey-Bass also publishes its books in a variety of electronic formats. Some content that appears in print may not be available in electronic books.

Cataloging-in-publication data has been applied for.
ISBN 978-0-4704-0435-5

Printed in the United States of America
FIRST EDITION
HB Printing   10 9 8 7 6 5 4 3 2 1

To Nikki, even more than before

Contents

TRUST ME

Introduction

Every communication is two conversations: the verbal one—the content—and the nonverbal one—the body language. If the two are aligned, you can be a persuasive, authentic communicator. You may even come across as charismatic. If the two are not aligned, people believe the nonverbal communication every time—and you will *not* seem authentic, even if you're just authentically nervous! People will believe that you're faking, or hiding something, or not completely present.

Most of us tend to think of the first conversation, the content, as the important one. We worry a lot about what to say when we're preparing for an important meeting, giving a big speech, or proposing marriage. And yet we rarely give as much thought to the second conversation: the body language. Then when the communication doesn't go well, we're surprised and don't understand why.

The reason is usually that our two conversations have been in conflict with one another. Our words were confident perhaps, but our body language—the second conversation— was nervous. And as research into how the brain works grows in depth and sophistication, we're coming to understand that what I'm calling the second conversation is actually more important in some ways than the first one.

We're still learning about the brain, but it is clear that our normal, everyday working model of it is a little outmoded. Most of us think that we're relatively rational beings. We get a thought, we decide to act on it, we instruct our bodies to move, and they do. So, for example, we wake up in the morning and think, "I need a cup of coffee." Our brain then instructs our body to go to the kitchen, prepare the coffee, get the mug out of the kitchen cabinet, and drink ourselves into wakefulness.

But it doesn't actually work that way much of the time. We get nonverbal impulses for a lot of the important things that drive us: relationships, safety, emotional needs, fears, desires, meeting new people, seeing old friends, and so on. Our bodies immediately start to act on these impulses, and *then*, a bit later, we form a conscious thought about what we're doing. It's as though our rational minds are explaining to ourselves after the fact why we're doing something. That intent comes from somewhere deep in the brain, beneath where conscious thought originates. And that intent, coming perhaps from what some call the limbic brain, governs a good deal of our supposedly rational lives.[1]

WE ARE ALL UNCONSCIOUS EXPERTS IN EACH OTHER'S BODY LANGUAGE

We are all unconscious experts at reading other people's body language. We learned this from a very early age, back when our lives depended on getting food, love, shelter, and dry diapers. Nevertheless, few of us are good at reading body language consciously. Instead, we get impressions and ascribe intent to the other person. We think to ourselves, *He doesn't like me very much*, or, *She's trying to cut me out*, or, *They really think I'm funny*. And it's at this level of intent that most of our own body language begins. If you put together this primacy of body language in many important areas of human concern, with our unconscious expertise at reading it, you get a paradox when you start to think about improving your abilities as a communicator.

Here's the rub. If you start to think hard about your body language because you want to control it and make it align with your content so that you're persuasive, authentic, and even charismatic, you run into a problem: you're thinking consciously about an unconscious activity, which slows your body language down and makes it happen just a bit late. The people around you, those unconscious experts, sense that something is wrong, but they can't put their fingers on the problem precisely. They'll think something like, *He didn't seem real*, or, *She looked fake—scripted or something*. They won't tell you the real problem—that your gestures and content are out of sync—because they're not consciously aware of what's going on.

It needs to go like this: *intent → gesture → thought → words*. If you try to control your body language at the level of conscious thought, it will come out like this: *thought → words → gesture*. And it will look all wrong.

That's a problem for any leader who knows that she has to communicate effectively on good days and bad, nervous or not, and prepared or not, and can't afford to show up looking inauthentic because she's thinking too hard about trying to appear real.

THE PROBLEM COMES WHEN YOU MAKE THE UNCONSCIOUS CONSCIOUS

The leader's behavior is also a problem for coaches, like me, who are expert at watching body language and want to advise you, "Don't cross your arms at that point in your presentation, because it will look defensive at a moment when you're talking about being open." If we coach you at the level of specific gestures, you'll make those conscious, they'll happen too slowly and out of sync with your thoughts, and you'll look fake.

As I've coached people over the years, my clients and I have wrestled with this problem. The solution has been to practice over and over again until the coordination of word and gesture becomes second nature, or almost so.

But thanks to recent brain research and my own continuing efforts to make teaching the two conversations as simple as possible, we can now resolve the paradox with another one. This change will greatly speed up the work of turning you into a powerful, persuasive, authentic, charismatic communicator, whether you're having a one-on-one meeting, engaging in a board-level discussion, or giving a speech to a thousand employees.

We are going to accomplish all this by having you work at the level of intent. The paradox is that you're going to be thinking both hard and consciously, but you'll resolve the problem by learning how to keep the work at an emotional level, like actors preparing for a role. This way, you'll be as close to the unconscious mind as possible, even though you are consciously thinking about your communication issues.

I have developed four steps, from simple to more complex, that you can take in order to learn to communicate authentically and charismatically. If you practice these four steps as intuitively as possible, without being too conscious about what you are doing, you'll find yourself easily resolving communications issues that may have bedeviled you for years. In addition, for those who want more detailed instruction, I lay out a series of principles of persuasive communication for both the content conversation and the gesture conversation. Take these as guidelines to use as they are appropriate for you. Different ones apply more powerfully at different times, and you can practice one and then another as you progress to become a more effective communicator.

Over and over again as I have worked with clients while developing this method, I have seen profound transformations happen quickly, even in a couple of hours. Introverted, ineffective communicators have learned to open up and take the stage with confidence and enthusiasm. It's exciting to watch and will work for you too.

The key is not to intellectualize too much the work you're going to do. Once you get the hang of it, it will seem easy. So take a deep breath, and jump in. Authenticity and charisma await you.

HOW THIS BOOK IS ORGANIZED

I've organized the book so that you can get to the practical application as quickly as possible. Chapters One and Two set out the theory. Chapters Three through Ten explain how to apply the theory to become an authentic and charismatic communicator. Chapter Eleven gives you a system to read others' intents. Chapters Twelve and Thirteen go deep into the research and set out the principles for those who are curious about the detail. And Chapter Fourteen concludes with some more information about our nonverbal conversations and how to control fear (in communicating) for those who are afflicted with it.

Leaders Need Both Charisma and Authenticity

Somewhere between the twentieth and the twenty-first centuries, the general public became tired of hype and decided that it wanted authenticity instead. It's the most important quality in leadership communications today. With it, you can move people to action. Without it, you can't even get a hearing.

And then there's charisma—the X factor every leader wants, even if some won't admit it. These are the ones who often say something like, "I'd rather just be me. That's more authentic." What they really mean by that is, *I don't want to do the hard work of practice. I'll just wing it.*

Are the two qualities really opposed? It is at the heart of this book to argue that you can have it both ways. In fact, in this era of nonstop communications and demands for authenticity from leaders, you have to be both charismatic and authentic to lead successfully for any length of time. And you have to practice hard to achieve apparently spontaneous authenticity and charisma. This book will show you how.

I'm assuming that you're a leader, or a leader in training, who wants to make sure that your communications—whether to one or many, formal or informal, prepared or off the cuff—are as persuasive, powerful, effective, authentic, and charismatic as possible. To reach that happy state, you have to be prepared to work on controlling your communications so that they are instrumental for your career and not merely subject to happenstance.

We'll begin with a little work on how people actually communicate, to clear away some common misunderstandings that get in the way of both charisma and authenticity.

EVERY COMMUNICATION IS TWO CONVERSATIONS

The first conversation in every communication is the one you're aware of: the content. The second conversation is the one that you're an unconscious expert on: the nonverbal one. These two always go together. In fact, they are so integral to one another that most people tend to gesture with their hands and change facial expression even when they're talking on the phone. No one else can see them, yet they keep gesturing on regardless. It's not just habit. There's a profound reason that people gesture when they attempt to communicate even when they can't be seen.

We tend to think that the second conversation is merely an accompaniment to the first. As we talk, we might wave our hands in the air, perhaps as a poor substitute or stand-in for content. We believe, if we ever think about it, that the gestures are just follow-ons: something to do with our hands; something that clarifies the meaning, or emphasizes something being said, or helps keep the other person listening; something that follows the words—maybe a physical flourish to enliven our sometimes less-than-thrilling content.

This way of thinking is profoundly wrong, and a chief aim of this book is to change it. All kinds of insights about how to communicate flow from getting it right.

GESTURE CAN CONVEY MEANING INDEPENDENT OF WORDS

Some people, on reflection, may admit that they sometimes gesture when they can't think of the words, or at least the right words, to say. Oddly enough, that's often sufficient for the other person to get the meaning intended. But rather than giving credit to the gesture for conveying the meaning, we usually give the other person credit for reading our minds, to our relief.

Try the following experiment in this context. Sit in a public place—perhaps a restaurant where the tables are close together and the conversation is lively. Sit with your back to a pair of people who are having an animated conversation. Listen hard, and try to capture as much of the meaning as you can. You will be surprised at how hard it is to follow the conversation. You will hear broken phrases, agreement to something you haven't caught, simultaneous talking, abrupt changes of topic you weren't expecting (but for some reason the speakers were), and apparently incoherent exchanges of information. If one person in the duo is dominating the conversation, perhaps telling elaborate stories, you may get more of it than you otherwise would. But if it's an average, reasonably equal exchange, you will be astonished at how fragmentary and elusive the communication is.

Why is that? The reason is that the "second conversation" is really the first. For certain kinds of communications, indeed most of the ones we really care about, we communicate first with the gesture and second with the word. This concept is central to this book.

There is a host of interesting implications from this insight, but for now, I'll say just that it means that when people communicate topics of great importance to them, they gesture what they mean a split second before the word comes out.

In fact, one way of looking at the brain contrasts our cerebral cortex with our limbic brain and suggests that certain kinds of gesture originate in the limbic a split second before the cortex fires away with its conscious thoughts. In other words, rather than thinking, *I'm hungry, so I'll pick up the bowl of soup now*, our brains direct the soup to be picked up unconsciously, and then form a conscious explanation of what we're doing (*I just picked up that cup because I'm hungry*).[1]

Why should we care about that? Because it turns the commonsense way we think about word and gesture upside down, and because those interesting implications flow from that inversion of common sense.

Gesture comes first. You can confirm this for yourself if you go back to the restaurant, this time keeping your eyes firmly trained on those two people in conversation and listening closely. Focus especially on gestures that accompany the noun phrases. Let's say one person says, "How did you get there?"

and the other responds, "I took an airplane." Watch the gesture associated with the word *airplane*. Depending on the information being conveyed, the gesture will start before the entire sentence or just before the word *airplane* itself. If there's strong attitude, such as something like, *Of course, I took an airplane; it's three thousand miles away over water. How else would I get there, you idiot?* then the gesture may convey all the emotional freight in the communiqué: the *Of course it's three thousand miles away over water how else would I get there you idiot* part. The person might shrug and turn her palms upward, while raising her eyebrows and looking hard at the interlocutor. She might shake her head and offer a half-smile. Those facial and hand gestures get across all the emotional meaning she wished to convey to her friend—maybe not in precisely those words, but close enough for both parties to get the message.

It's the nature of most of our communications that they unroll like this one. We use surprisingly few words and convey the emotional colors and tones of the conversation mostly through gesture.

When two people know each other well, gesture can take up a larger part of the communications between them. In this regard, it becomes a kind of shortcut that allows the two to alert one another to important shifts in the conversation or strong feelings or topics to avoid. When two lovers meet, for example (not the ones in movies who have just fallen in love, but those who have had an intimate relationship for a long time), a touch, a few murmured words, and a kiss may convey all that needs to be said about a day, a meeting, or an important issue that has been pending between them.

Love is expressed primarily through gesture: a look, an arch of the eyebrow, a touch, a kiss.

OUR MOST IMPORTANT DIALOGUES WITH OTHERS TAKE PLACE NONVERBALLY

Many of our dialogues with others, and most of our important ones, take place nonverbally. Portions of them are unconscious.

So gesture comes first, and it conveys most of the emotion that a communication intends. In addition to emotion, certain other basic things are conveyed. Relationships, spatial distances between people, physical motion and place in general, basic needs like food, shelter, sex, and so on: all of these are first gesture conversations, then only secondarily, and later, content conversations. Think of it as everything that a smart cave man and woman would need to get along on a typical busy day defending the hearth, slaying woolly mammoths, raising the kids, and creating cave paintings in the few minutes at the end of the day that a cave person can call his or her own.

What else is going on?

This is a good place to talk about a seminal study in the communication world—one that is frequently misquoted and misunderstood. It's time to get it right.

HOW IS INTENT SIGNALED THROUGH GESTURE?

Almost forty years ago, Albert Mehrabian, one of the pioneers of communications research, undertook a small-scale study about how people signal and decode the attitude toward the words they were uttering and hearing.[2] In other words, if a person says the word *love*, does he say it like someone in love, or someone who has been betrayed by love, or someone who thinks love is for saps? And how do we know?

What Mehrabian found was that in order to decode the emotions underlying words, audiences look to visual cues—the gestures—55 percent of the time, the tone of voice 38 percent of the time, and the content only 7 percent of the time. This conclusion shocked people then and continues to shock today, but the implications are even more important than most typically realize.

What's really going on is that the emotional freight of any communication begins in gesture, is conveyed mostly by gesture, and can even remain as gesture—unspoken and sometimes even unconscious. That's because the limbic brain is where the important emotions originate, and the gestures are our primary way of expressing them. Conscious thought comes later, and words come later still. It's what we mean by "gut feel" and all those moments when we can't articulate something, but we just know it.

UNCONSCIOUS THOUGHT IS FASTER AND MORE EFFICIENT THAN CONSCIOUS THOUGHT

As a species, we're always trying to articulate our feelings and tell people to get in touch with them, and so on, but in fact they're doing quite well unconsciously. Unconscious thought is fast and efficient. It's just that it isn't conscious.

Here's the next implication of this line of research. Two people, or a leader and her audience, can have an unconscious communication that is entirely composed of gestures of various kinds and realize that consciously only later, or not at all.

THE TWO CONVERSATIONS DON'T HAVE TO
BE CONNECTED

When I say that every communication is two conversations, both verbal and nonverbal, I mean that precisely. They don't have to have an immediate, obvious connection, although they often do. Think about the exchange between two people where one is bearing very bad news to the other. The bearer may gesture strong signals of comfort, love, and solidarity while quietly stating the shattering news in a simple, unadorned way.

Although the two conversations are connected, they are proceeding along two parallel tracks, and it is easier to see how the gesture is not merely an afterthought to the words. In fact, that kind of communication usually begins with a reassuring gesture or look, which alerts the recipient that bad news is coming.

Think too about when two people are carrying on a flirtation under the noses of their colleagues while talking about meeting the second-quarter quotas, for example. There, the two conversations are unrelated, to the great private amusement of the flirters.

That's rather a lot to get from Mehrabian—more than he did—but it is important to clear the ground of misconception. Mehrabian understood that he was trying to see how emotional subtext was decoded, but his study has been misinterpreted ever since as being about how meaning is decoded. That has led to all sorts of silly commentary along the lines that "it doesn't matter what you say, it's how you look." That's not what the study showed at all, but that's the way it has been taken.

What the study showed was that people decode emotions primarily through gesture (and tone of voice). What I'm claiming now, based on more recent research and my work with clients, is that the emotional component represents a separate nonverbal conversation that is parallel to the verbal one and typically occurs a split-second before the verbal one.

MASTER BOTH CONVERSATIONS, ESPECIALLY THE SECOND

It's the nonverbal conversation that will make or break you as a communicator. It may confirm you as the top dog, sabotage your authority, connect you with your mate for life, get you in a fistfight (or out of one), win you a game or lose one, blow your chances at getting a raise or get you the big sale, lose you the prize or win it—and on and on through most of the big moments in life.

How can you become more aware of this conversation that your body is having with the other bodies around you? Is it worth the effort? Will you become self-conscious and inauthentic if you do? Can you monitor what everyone else is "saying"? Is that helpful? Will it get you to places you won't otherwise reach?

Understanding the second conversation is key to leadership today, because it's not something that you can leave to chance or the unconscious. There are simply too many decisions to be made, too many inputs to weigh, too many players to manage and lead. In the twenty-first century, the pace of leadership has accelerated, the flow of information has exploded, and the sheer physical and intellectual demands on leaders have intensified. You can't rely on common sense or instinct or winging it today as you once might have done.

THE CAMERA IS ALWAYS ON YOU

With camcorders and YouTube everywhere, you have to assume that your life as a leader is almost entirely transparent. This relentless scrutiny means that your decisions are subject to endless second-guessing after the fact. Most of life is now subject to the instant replay. How good will you look in slow motion?

Leaders who rely on ad-libbing and improvisation risk looking unprepared and stilted. The irony of leadership in the media age is that winging it looks fake; only the prepared can look authentic.

This raises the stakes on our cave person communication skills. It's time to learn how to control the nonverbal conversation as well as we control the content discussions of our lives. It's time to stop leaving the emotional side of leadership to chance. It's time to make ourselves aware of our own and others' need for the second conversation—the physical messages our limbic brains send out faster than we can think about ourselves, our surroundings, and the others in our lives. If you can accomplish that, you can boost your leadership skills, increase your authority, and intensify your personal charisma.

WHAT IS CHARISMA?

There are a lot of myths and misconceptions about charisma. The dictionary definition is " 'a capacity to inspire devotion and enthusiasm; aura' from the Greek 'kharis' meaning favor or grace."[3] In practice, people usually take it to mean that a person with charisma is someone you can't take your eyes off of, someone who's really interesting.

Charisma is several things. First, there's awareness that others are looking at you. When you have that awareness, you hold yourself differently. Remember the way you felt the last time you were in front of an audience? That kind of heightened awareness is the trick to exuding charisma when you walk into a room. If you believe that people are looking at you, they probably are.

Second, and most important, it's expressiveness of a wide array of strong emotions. Think of an actor who exudes charisma. Jack Nicholson, for example, can go from laughter to rage to a terrifying loony scariness in a matter of seconds, and often does.

This is the hard part for most business leaders, who have been trained to keep their cool and not to display emotion. And of course part of leadership is tactfulness: knowing when to act in one way or another. Most leaders don't have the freedom of Jack Nicholson. Nonetheless, a range of appropriate emotions is an important part of charisma. And it's also a large part of what we think of as authenticity today. That's why organizations hire celebrities as spokespeople and put them in the rather ridiculous position of giving their opinions on everything under the sun. We equate expressiveness with authenticity. Precisely because we're often unconscious of our emotions, when we see a lot of them coming from someone else, with some control nonetheless, we think they're authentic.

Third, it's an element of enjoyment at being the center of attention. As I said in my book *Working the Room*, the secret to good speechmaking is to enjoy yourself.[4] Of course, that's easier said than done, but if you have no appetite for the limelight, you have no business in leadership today. The same is true of communications in general. Part of charisma is conveying zest at the game—a wink and a nod to show that you're not taking it all too seriously. Pomposity is fatal for charisma.

And fourth, it's an ability to surprise us. We have no idea what charismatic people will do next. That's why we watch them. Remember Tom Cruise on Oprah's couch. You may have thought he was crazy, but you didn't take your eyes off him. That's charisma, though he had to work pretty hard to get it. A leader wouldn't want to appear that crazy—but nevertheless would want to retain a little of that edginess that goes with the occasional surprise. The alternative is boredom.

WHAT IS AUTHENTICITY?

Authenticity is a little more complicated. A whole range of people, from Barack Obama to the Shoe Bomber, can be said to be authentic. It has to do with the frank expression of emotion of some kind, whether positive or negative. We believe people are authentic when they are open with us in a sense that feels real. It has to do with transparency of motive and intention. We believe people are authentic when we know what makes them tick—because they've told us and their actions bear it out. And it has to do with consistency of action. We believe that people are authentic when they keep the same agenda for a substantial period of time. A more elegant way to say this is that we believe people are authentic when they show us their hearts. Because that's most often with some strong emotion, expressiveness becomes a proxy for authenticity in our shortcut-prone age.

But if I were to ask you to stand up and be authentic, you would look at me with a mixture of trepidation and annoyance. You wouldn't know how to do it. I know, because I've tried this as an opening gambit in seminars I've taught on charisma and authenticity. Yet by the end of the day, after the participants have learned the four basic steps to becoming authentic and charismatic, when I ask them to stand up and be authentic, they can.

Once you've read this book, you'll know how to accomplish this feat as well. Then it's just a matter of doing it.

Aligning the Two Conversations Will Make You a Powerful Communicator

So we have two conversations, one verbal and the other nonverbal. The nonverbal one covers emotions and relationships and threats to safety and a variety of other things that are usually unconscious, and happen first. We think it happens the other way around, but that's precisely because thinking is the conscious part.

When the two conversations are aligned, a communication can be persuasive, powerful, and consistent. When they're not aligned, people believe the nonverbal conversation every time.[1] If that seems hard to believe, a simple example will convince you.

Imagine a speaker walking to the front of the room. You can tell that he has no energy. His shoulders are a little bowed, perhaps, and he's not moving very fast. His head may be pointing down. When he gets to the front, he turns to the audience. He doesn't make eye contact but rather looks over everyone's head. He folds his arms defensively over his chest and then moves back a couple of paces. Finally, he says, "I'm really glad to be here today."

What do you do now? If you're honest, you're reaching for your BlackBerry or your day planner. You may even be looking for an exit. You're thinking, *Oh, dear. This is not going to be good.*

That's the power of unaligned communications.

Aligning the verbal and the nonverbal gets you the audience's attention and an open mind, at least for a few minutes. After that, it's up to you.

It's the same deal in a one-on-one conversation with a direct report. The staff member may shuffle in to your office without making eye contact with you, sit down with a thump and a sigh, and, in response to your question, "How's it going on the Q report?" say, "It's fine."

WE UNCONSCIOUSLY ASCRIBE INTENT TO THE GESTURES WE SEE

In the conversation with the employee, unless you're completely clueless, you know you've got trouble with the Q report. You may not have even noticed the precise physical things that employee did to convince you of this. What we all do, as unconscious experts of nonverbal communication of emotions, is ascribe intent to what we see. We don't think to ourselves, *Oh, I see a slumped shoulder and a bowed head. I sense trouble.* Instead, we jump immediately to intent, decoding what we see: *Uh-oh, Jones is in trouble. This could be bad.*

That's precisely because this expertise developed over eons in order to keep us alive and functioning in the tribe. We had to learn to respond instantly to nonverbal cues because by the time they became conscious, it might have been too late.

Our reactions can be largely nonverbal and emotional and can even stay in the unconscious. That's a good thing in the cave. It's less useful in the modern era, when we have to do civilized things like lead thousands of people to action, manage groups of employees, and have conversations with discouraged coworkers.

Here, our natural tendencies to self-preservation can get in the way. Defensiveness, which makes perfect sense when you are about to have a confrontation with a saber-tooth tiger, creates a bad feeling when you are trying to lead a team of software engineers. Fight-or-flight reactions of hostility, rapid heart rates, and flared nostrils don't serve us well when the boss says, "How are you going to accomplish X in time frame Y?" They would have been fine when fleeing a woolly mammoth, but it's no longer the case.

OUR INSTINCT FOR SELF-PRESERVATION CAN BETRAY US

Because our instincts can betray us, we have to learn how to manage them. We must be able to have the two conversations together in a controlled, useful, *conscious* way. That's the essence of leadership communications, and it's a tall order. How can we make the unconscious conscious without losing spontaneity, power, and the appearance of ease?

I have coached many people over the twenty-three years I've been in the business. Until I had the breakthrough that forms the basis of this book, I always taught the relevant bits of communications theory in order to explain to my clients why it was important to master their posture, or their hand gestures, or the expressions that play across their face, or the way they move in relation to the audience, and so on. What I've observed is that the really good ones take in the information quickly and are able to add it to their repertoire of activities in a fluid and natural way. The folks who struggle are the ones who are in over their heads anyway.

But it has always nagged at me that there ought to be a way to teach authenticity and charisma without making people self-conscious first and therefore less able to communicate fluidly, before they can become expert and fluent once again. And even some of the good ones relapse and return to old behavior at times because they're under stress, or tired, or working on something new.

I worked once with a consultant who was going to give a series of speeches around the world on a study he had just completed. The speech was quite difficult to construct because of the enormous amount of data to digest and present in a way that was interesting to his audiences. But we found a way to make the material clear and lively, and it was time to rehearse. The consultant understood the ideas I was sharing with him about how to work with an audience, and he realized (when he watched his recorded performance) that he was using some gestures that were not aligned with his message and getting in the way of connecting with the audience. He quickly improved and received his first standing ovation ever on the first delivery of the speech.

And yet at a follow-up rehearsal, we both realized that he was fighting the tendency to revert to his old behavior, at least during practice. As a smart consultant, he was already thinking about his next client and new content. He wasn't "present" at the rehearsal. The result was that the contradiction showed up in a mismatch between his body language and content. It was very discouraging for him, as a perfectionist, and alarming for me as a coach, to think that he was slipping backward.

It wasn't until the performance of the material in front of a new audience that he found the necessary concentration and focus to deliver on his improved alignment of content and gesture.

THINK ABOUT YOUR INTENT, NOT YOUR GESTURE

In exploring these paradoxes of the twenty-first century, where ease must be studied and learned, where artlessness looks clumsy, where natural is fake and artifice seems real, I hit on a way to bypass the conscious trap of thinking about gesture. It's a trap because conscious thought is slower than physical thought and to reverse the process looks fake to anyone. It's the old joke of the sound and picture being slightly out of sync in the movie, which instantly turns high art into farce. But if we think about the intent behind the gesture rather than the gesture, we can leave the limbic brain to do its work at the speed only it can achieve. And then we can look natural and convincing while controlling the second conversation.

This is not easy work, and it involves necessarily a paradox: thinking about *not* thinking about something. But it is possible, because it involves a different kind of thinking. Actors who practice the so-called Method developed by Constantin Stanislavsky work on finding the emotional truth that gives rise to the action rather than the more traditional schools that taught actors how to move, speak, and gesture.[2] The idea is that you dig deep into your memories to find a powerful moment when you were afraid, say, in order to conjure up the actions that you would naturally take when afraid, rather than choosing from among some stock gestures that traditionally indicate fear.

The work that we're going to undertake in this book has somewhat different activities and aims, but it is fundamentally similar. The goal is to sidestep your natural human tendency to think consciously about what you're doing when you're, say, going to an interview with the boss. The result of that conscious thought is that you get nervous and then you don't handle the interview well—the opposite of your intent in thinking about it. Instead you focus on being open, if that's the main thing you're worried about in front of the boss, so that you won't become defensive. You picture in your mind someone you're comfortable with, say, a spouse or close friend. You imagine a conversation with that person and note the body language that goes with it. (You're not going to kiss your boss, of course.) You practice that body language until it becomes natural. You add the imagined conversation with the boss on top of that, keeping the open body language as you develop and practice the content. You note how that feels.

Now you're ready to make that long walk down the hall to the boss's office. Along the way, you're getting into the mind-set that you've rehearsed and running over the first lines of your conversation. And then you knock on the door.

If that seems like a lot of work, consider the alternatives. This whole process takes maybe an hour of preparation. If you do it right, it will ensure as much as is humanly possible that you will remain confident and open in front of your boss during the interview. Consider what that's worth to you.

That's basically it. Once you understand how communication between people really works and you get that it's two conversations—one of which is the content and largely conscious, and the other of which is nonverbal and mostly unconscious—then there are only a few major steps to take to achieve mastery over your communications.

The next step to think about is how to get control of that unconscious process. In fact, you may well wonder, *Why should I bother to do all the work? It sounds difficult, and besides, it will only make me look clumsy and artificial. I agree that leaders today need to be authentic and charismatic, but how will this help?*

THE PARADOX OF LEADERSHIP IS THAT YOU HAVE TO PRACTICE TO LOOK SPONTANEOUS

Here's where the paradox of leadership comes in. I've seen this over and over again in my work with executives, politicians, and professional speakers. Because we humans tend to interpret fumbling, hesitations, and sloppiness as evidence of lack of preparedness, inauthenticity, and amateurishness, the communicators who wing it instead of preparing always fail to impress. The ones who rehearse, role-play, and prepare with real passion are the ones who connect with their public, their audiences, and their followers.

In part, the increasing sophistication of the nonstop news cycle and Internet-addicted audience has created this paradox. We're used to intimate conversations of celebrities and newsmakers in the cozy world of our daily television fare. We expect that what's said at a conference or a press appearance or after an important meeting will be shown on CNN or YouTube within minutes.

The glare of the klieg lights on leadership in the business world, politics, and education is pitiless, unending, and intolerant of amateurs. A CEO can literally destroy a company with some ill-chosen words in front of the TV cameras and microphones while commenting on how something went horribly wrong at a plant, with a product, or in the last financial quarter.

And yet, at the same time, and in part because leaders have so often let us down in recent years with inauthentic behavior and deception (think Enron, WorldCom, Mattel, and others), we demand authenticity and the appearance of honest, open communications. When the lights go on and the crisis is in full play, we are ready to judge the performance of our leaders in an instant. Are they relaxed, casual, honest, and emotional—and simultaneously commanding, to the point, and authoritative? If they are, they can live to communicate another day. But if they are hesitant, self-contradictory, or disengaged, they're toast.

WE WANT LEADERS WHO LOOK REAL

We want authentic people as leaders today, and what the world doesn't realize is how hard it is to appear that way. It takes understanding of how communications works, and it takes practice. There's nothing spontaneous about authenticity in this televised age.

Over the years, I have coached many executives who want to bring their game up to this high level of play. I've taught them what's crucial, according to the research, to appear effective in public, in meetings, and in all the other situations in which leaders must communicate. Content must be presented in specific ways for people to hear what you want them to hear. And the nonverbal conversation must be conveyed in the right voice, with the right posture, gestures, and motion.

Clients have sometimes complained that I've made them worse before they've gotten better because the burden of self-knowledge is at first overwhelming. They ask me, "How can I worry about my voice, my posture, my gestures, and motion while at the same time thinking about what I'm saying, and—by the way—paying attention to the audience's reception of all this input?"

One CEO told me that he'd need "six heads" to keep track of all that was going on. In time and with lots of practice, he changed his story. There was a gratifying moment a few months into our work together when it clicked for him, and he came back from a high-level meeting with other CEOs and the president of the United States saying, "I did it! I nailed it!"

THERE IS A SIMPLE WAY TO MASTER
THE TWO CONVERSATIONS

Part of my quest to understand communications has included an effort to find a simple way to teach mastery of the two conversations. Not everyone has the patience, and not everyone is willing to make the time, to master their voice, posture, gestures, and motion, as well as content and audience interaction and "reading." And, in truth, it's the nonverbal aspect of communications that is particularly hard to master, precisely because it is largely unconscious.

In my work recently with clients, I've broken down authenticity and charisma into four discrete steps that, when practiced individually and rolled up together, provide a simple, nontechnical way for leaders to achieve mastery of the demands of modern communications. Mastery of the first two steps will make you authentic, and mastery of the second two will give you charisma.

In the rest of this book, I set out the four steps in depth, why we need this kind of approach, and the research behind it, so that you can work through it in your everyday life. Some people, of course, benefit more from practicing some of the steps than others. You may already be a master of one or more of them, but few will be a master of all four.

Step One: Being Open   Your first task is to approach an audience, a meeting, or an interview as if you were comfortably at home talking to a loved one or a friend with whom you're very relaxed. The point is to imagine the encounter, practice it, note the nonverbal gestures that go with it, and then use this same body language when you're in the less intimate setting. The overall idea is to relax and achieve an open stance so that you look at least as comfortable as, say, David Letterman on his talk show.

Step Two: Being Connected   Now you focus on your audience, whether it's one person or many. Your nonverbal posture orients toward them, and you zero in on their issues and problems. As with openness, this is at once a question of message and body language, content and delivery. Continuing the role play from the first step, you might imagine you were trying to get the attention of your four year old, who is engaged with some TV show. What would you say? How would you act? Would you draw nearer to your child? Get down at her level? Grab her arm? How can you translate that strong connection into the lukewarm one you have with, say, your direct reports at work?

Step Three: Being Passionate   Here, you concentrate on your own feelings and emotions. How do you connect with the subject matter at hand? What do you want or feel toward it? What's your underlying emotion during the encounter— not the irritation you might feel about a direct report who's giving you excuses about why a project is going to be late, but rather your passion for the project itself? Once you know what that underlying emotion is, how do you show it? What's your repertoire of emotions at work? Can you imagine expanding them?

Emotions are interesting; it's why we watch TV avidly when disaster happens even though we know we shouldn't. Marshall McLuhan famously analyzed television as a "cool" medium that craves emotion to make it hot.[3] The business world is like that too. So much of it is kept under emotional wraps that when someone does have an outburst, it is fascinating to watch and compelling to talk about at the water cooler. Those sorts of moments are remembered for a long time.

Step Four: Listening Finally, authentic and charismatic communication requires that you listen to your audience. What is the underlying emotion of the person in front of you? Do you know what it is? If not, why not? During the course of the meeting, the event, the conference, or the speech, what's the journey you want to take that person or persons on? Where do they start, and where do you want them to end?

. . .

These four steps are simple yet profound. Achieving each step, however, is not necessarily simple. You may have to fight years of practice at being closed with your colleagues and subordinates, for example. That kind of learned body language is hard to change. But if you approach this effort with the intent of being open rather than trying to control the specific behavior, you'll find that your nonverbal behavior will change automatically to go along with your new intent.

You'll discover something else surprising too: the new body language will change your own thinking. When you adopt open behavior, you'll find yourself thinking more open thoughts. In fact, you will become more authentic. This sounds paradoxical, but it's the natural result of the way our minds work. Recall that conscious thought comes more slowly than the emotional language of our bodies. So when our bodies are telling us that we're open, our thoughts naturally follow.

There's lots more to be said about these four steps: how they're done, what pitfalls to avoid, how to manage not to look like an idiot when you're trying new things, and so on.

That's the detail explained in subsequent chapters. But for now, it's enough to note that as I've worked with clients, it's been extraordinary to see the breakthroughs as they've put these four simple steps together to bring about some profound changes in their behavior and thinking.

Each step demands a more thoughtful stance toward all your communications than you may be used to. You can't listen in the moment to a colleague with any real mindfulness or attention without having done a great deal of work to understand him beforehand. As you're watching nonverbal behavior, you can't evaluate it successfully unless you already know the individual in question. What does that little characteristic twist of the hand mean when Jim is thinking? Is it a sign that he's not agreeing with you—or did he injure his hand playing tennis the week before?

I make one final claim before we dive into the detail: this work is therapeutic in many cases. You'll find it healing to work on being open, connected, passionate, and a good listener. If you're already all those things, you'll get even better. But for most of us, our workaday worlds are the place where we put our emotional lives on hold. Opening up in this context may seem weak, or risky, or even foolish to some, but that's because they're thinking in twentieth-century ways about work and communication. In fact, changes in the workplace, society, and culture have made it essential that twenty-first century leaders learn how to become authentic and charismatic, and this is the only way to accomplish it.

Being Open, Part One

How to Master the Verbal Conversation

Being open is the ante for any kind of successful leadership communication in the twenty-first century. Consumers, the public, audiences, analysts, employees, or anyone else you might talk to or meet with have such highly developed filters for detecting what is real and what is merely hype that you can't afford not to be transparent and authentic in your communications. It begins with openness.

WHAT IT MEANS TO BE OPEN AND HOW TO DO IT

There are verbal and nonverbal aspects to openness. This chapter is about the verbal side of things, and the next is about the nonverbal.

Consider the following precepts as guidelines for achieving openness. You won't be able to follow all of them all the time as a leader, but together they will serve you well. They are based on my experience of studying the communications research, working with clients, and teaching at four universities.

Fundamentally, openness is a willingness to acknowledge all facets of your persona—to own everything without defensiveness and with honesty about intent.

One of the many ironies of public life today is that the secrets you try hardest to keep will almost certainly be revealed sooner or later. Furthermore, the public will be interested in them only to the extent that you continue to conceal your intent behind your actions. As soon as the human context is clear and we understand fully, we begin to move on.

At this writing, to pick a typically sordid example, the revelations of former New York governor Eliot Spitzer's involvement in a prostitution ring dominate the headlines. They will fascinate us as long as Spitzer himself is not forthcoming about his intent. As soon as he puts a story behind the actions—let's say he tells us that he has a secret weakness for wannabe singers or a self-destructive urge because he feels worthless inside—then we will shake our heads wisely and turn the page.

Clarity of Intent   As humans, we believe that actions, especially ones directed toward us, are meaningful, and we want to know the meanings. Children learn early to ask, "Why?" until their parents run out of answers. They are trying to delve into and broaden their understanding of intent.

Because intent is so important to us as humans, clarity of intent lies at the very heart of being open. If I know what you intend, I can understand you, and my willingness to be open to you increases. The simplest way to be clear about your intent is to tell me early in our communications together.

Language That Takes Responsibility Rather Than Evading It "Mistakes were made" is a classic way politicians use to apologize or admit errors without actually doing so. That's a passive construction that leaves the crucial actor, the politician, out of it. Unfortunately, we all know what he really means, so once again the politician reveals more than he intends by attempting to conceal. And we assume the worst. Open language therefore favors active verbs.

Framing the Context The first questions on everyone's minds when people communicate are about the whys of the meeting or event or conversation: *Why are we here? Why is this important? Why is this relevant to me?* We are trying to frame the encounter, whether it's a negotiation, a keynote speech, or an intimate conversation. Our first need is to be oriented, and we can't begin to pay attention to anything else until that's taken care of.

So answer your audience's need to know why, and do it quickly, simply, and directly. Clear, honest framing is essential for open communication. If you fail to create the context, that question will dog the proceedings from then on. And if you're duplicitous about the context, then when the betrayal comes, it will be fatal to trust and the possibility of further open communications.

Agreeing on the Agenda In casual communications, this step is accomplished quickly and effortlessly because of understandings that already exist. When two friends meet, for example, one will say, "Wassup?" to the other, and the conversation will pick up where it left off. Indeed, it will take a conscious effort in reframing to move the conversation off its usual tracks if one of the conversationalists wants to talk about something serious or different from the normal course of affairs.

In more formal settings, a good communicator knows that openness requires agreement on the agenda in order to avoid problems and recriminations later. The phrase, "You never told me that . . ." is a listener's way of registering that an agenda item was not agreed on. The danger is that when the other person says that, he is letting himself off the moral hook, at least to some extent. You may be stuck with the problem and the blame.

When an issue has been announced, briefly discussed, and added to the agenda, it becomes everyone's issue. If it is sprung as a surprise later, it will be your problem and your fault. The more intimate the relationship is, the more like a betrayal it will seem. Everyone (until they learn better) has had the experience of neglecting to tell a spouse or significant other some vital bit of information.

For example, you go to a party where the host is about to move to Bora-Bora. You forget to tell your spouse that vital detail, who finds out what everyone else knows at the shindig. Brace yourself for an indignant, "Why didn't you tell me!" on the car ride home.

WHEN THERE ARE DISAGREEMENTS BETWEEN THE PARTIES

In deeply contentious communications, where both sides have profound disagreements, not to acknowledge them up front commits a sin against openness and greatly decreases the likelihood of reaching any ultimate agreement.

Parties who fail to acknowledge the other side's strongly held beliefs seem to say, "I don't respect you enough to listen or articulate your position." You're indicating that you don't take it seriously when really all you may want to do is avoid contention.

Most of the verbal sins against openness are like this. It's hard to be open about contentious issues, and when we're not, we make the issues even more so. So we can all agree that it's better to be open; the problem is that it takes courage.

WHEN NOT TO BE COMPLETELY OPEN

Openness makes us good communicators and bad poker players. There are, of course, times when it's not appropriate to be completely open. In those cases, make sure the stakes are worth the gamble, because if it doesn't work out, trust will be gone and the possibility of communicating at all will end.

In this sense, rhetorical openness is an insurance policy against future communication losses and a policy worth taking. But it goes against the instincts of too many leaders to be open, take responsibility, admit to less-than-perfect intent, own a problem, or sign on to a solution that has risk and difficulty associated with it. We have to fight these tendencies if we're to be open communicators. In the long run, we will do much better communicating this way, but sometimes the long run looks very far off.

The examples of corporations that failed to be open under duress or a catastrophic event litter the organizational graveyards and casualty lists. Enron, WorldCom, Merck: the count goes on. On the other side, companies that manage to be open thrive and become heroes. The Tylenol scare was perhaps the first modern example of a company that survived in good part because the CEO and his team took the position of being completely open with the press. After the 1982 murders, sales of Tylenol collapsed, but with tamper-proof packaging in place, the brand recovered to 92 percent of its former sales within a few years, and it still retains a 35 percent market share in North America more than twenty-five years later.[1]

Openness in the verbal conversation continues with regular checking in with the other party to see how the exchange is going and allow a change of ground rules, subject, or other conditions if either party finds that necessary or desirable. If that sounds too obvious, think about meetings you've attended where someone dominated the agenda, railroaded an issue through despite opposition, or refused to give up when a cause was clearly lost. Remember how irritated you were? That's what it's like to experience closed conversation.

Where is the line between an irritating stubbornness and a principled, courageous refusal to give in to the prevailing political winds? It comes down to intent. A communicator who is transparent about her intent almost always gets more respect and tolerance from listeners than someone who isn't. But to achieve that kind of openness and to make it real, you have to be transparent about your values, not just your opinions. You have to say something on the order of, "I believe that justice is slow but inevitable, and so I am willing to wait as long as it takes for justice to be done." That kind of statement may not win you the love of your more impatient interlocutors, but it will earn you their respect and (perhaps grudging) forbearance for a while.

CONCLUDING AN OPEN COMMUNICATION

An open conversation concludes with reaching agreement about what has been said or negotiated, discussing any necessary follow-up and the dates and other details of the next communications, and some final words to wrap up. If this sounds like good manners or good business practices, it is. Much of what is considered good manners has to do with finding appropriate ways to communicate what needs to be said for good relations to continue, whether it's between people, organizations, or countries.

Beyond the basics that manners and good business teach us, though, there is something more fundamental going on. Openness about the procedural matters of a communication allows both parties to check substantive issues at the same time without offense. "So what we've agreed to is . . ." may sound awkward and intrusive if the communication has not been open until that point, but it will flow smoothly if discussions of process have been held all along. In some cases, process questions can even derail a delicate negotiation that has hitherto not entertained such issues.

I once worked for a consulting firm that taught all employees to end every meeting with a discussion of "benefits and concerns" resulting from the meeting. It was a chance to talk about what had gone right, what had not, and what needed to happen next. This took only a few moments at the end of a meeting and was well worth the effort. The formal aspects of communication are worth maintaining, because they allow openness to thrive within them.

Being Open, Part Two

How to Master the Nonverbal Conversation

In some ways, the nonverbal conversation is even more important to openness than the verbal. It's also important that the two conversations align here because an open verbal conversation coupled with a closed nonverbal conversation will create deep mistrust and discomfort in the other party.

THE ESSENTIAL GOAL: TRUST

Trust is the essential goal of an open nonverbal conversation. And it is the basis of so much in communications that it's worth saying a little more about it.

The essence of trust is believing that the other party will do what he or she says and that there are no nasty surprises coming. Trust is difficult to create and almost impossible to reestablish once it has been lost. Nonetheless, since so much of the second conversation is unconscious for most people, trust can be created, and recreated, almost imperceptibly by communicators who know what they are doing and who pay close attention to the details. I'll discuss the details first and then how to achieve them.

THE PHYSICAL COMPONENTS OF OPENNESS

Consider the physical activities one person can undertake to indicate openness to another. Most of us have had the importance of eye contact drummed into our heads. Looking people in the eye is supposed to indicate straightforward intentions, and not looking people in the eye the opposite. Unfortunately, as communications researcher Paul Ekman has established, it's not as simple as that.[1] As he points out, it is all too easy to control where you look; in fact, it's just about the easiest facial activity to control, and the face is easier to control than most other parts of the body.

An averted gaze signals a number of emotions: downward with sadness, down or away with shame or guilt, and away with disgust. Yet even the guilty liar probably won't avert his eyes much, since liars know that everyone expects to be able to detect deception in this way. Ekman thinks that blinking, pupil dilation, and tears are more reliable indicators of concealed emotion than mere gaze. These are more difficult for people to control willfully; indeed pupil dilation is involuntary. Concealed emotion itself is not necessarily an indication that someone is lying, but it is certainly an indication of a lack of openness. More generally, opened eyes and dilated pupils indicate interest, arousal, or excitement, and thus they are symptomatic of openness of various kinds.

Beyond the eyes, there are many clues to openness or its opposite in the rest of the face. The basic components are the eyebrows, the mouth, and the head itself, raising, smiling, and nodding, respectively. As Ekman and other have pointed out, these basic facial gestures, once thought to be culture based, have turned out to be virtually universal among humans and even primates. Couple them with a few more, like shaking the head no or frowning, and you have a near-universal grammar of the basic facial expression of emotion. The good news is that this grammar is made up of a relatively small set of terms.[2]

Of course, the face is capable of hundreds of gradations and variations of expressions, but these four—open eyes, raised eyebrows, nodding, and smiling—are the important ones to think about with respect to openness. We raise our eyebrows when we recognize someone in a brief flash, called, appropriately enough, the *eyebrow flash*. Holding the eyebrows up is a sign of openness because it invites response, queries the other person, or indicates surprise, depending on the arrangement of the rest of the face.

Smiling, of course, transforms the face. A real smile is infinitely more inviting and open than any other arrangement of the facial muscles. It's infectious, and it makes the person doing the smiling more attractive to everyone else.

Finally, nodding builds agreement, and so it helps with openness. President Bill Clinton made great use of the nod on the campaign trail and in debates with President George H. W. Bush in the 1992 election. He would take a question and begin to answer it by moving toward the listener. Once he got to the edge of the stage or camera range, he would plant his feet and then keep his eyes fixed on the questioner as he answered. As he concluded his answer, he would nod once or twice with his eyes still fixed on the questioner, and then move back to his stool. It was a highly effective way to show empathy, build trust, and create a sense of openness.

Beyond the face, the rest of the body has its own physical components of openness. Broadly speaking, we get closer to people we are open with and farther away from people we are not. This general rule also governs the activities of the hands and arms. We reach toward people we are open with and instinctively away from people we are not.[3] The Western custom of shaking hands allows relative strangers to touch hands without bringing the rest of their bodies too close together. And it shows whether the other person has any weapons concealed in his or her hands. It's a sign of greeting and of establishing a relationship. Of course, it doesn't mean much beyond that, but if someone won't shake hands with us, we are right to be worried or suspicious. It's a gesture that is more noticeable in its absence than its presence.

Keep your eye on the other hand too; that's often more revealing than the hand that does the shaking. If it's clenched, concealed, or otherwise not simply hanging down by the thigh, then there may well be some concealed emotion or intention implied. The double handshake, where the second hand is brought up and placed on the forearm or over the other hand, is powerful precisely because it relieves us of a nagging worry about the other hand.

More important, perhaps, is the action of the torso. We turn our torsos toward people we wish to be open with and keep them turned away from those we don't. The heart is what's at stake, of course: we don't feel comfortable leaving our hearts exposed for long if there is no trust or openness.

People use their hands and arms to protect the heart and torso when they don't feel comfortable being open. We see this kind of behavior in public speaking constantly when we have a speaker who folds his arms defensively over his heart when talking about how great the future looks for the audience, or the speaker who folds her hands over her stomach while expressing optimism about sales in the next quarter. Neither speaker realizes the extent to which the content of the presentation is undercut by the nonverbal behavior. Most audiences don't register these subtleties consciously. Instead, they form a general impression of the intent of the speaker, since that's what matters to them. So an audience will decide that the two speakers in the previous paragraph were not being open without ever knowing consciously why they made the decision that the speaker lacked authority, or conviction, or something of the sort.

Our unconscious expertise at reading body language gives us that much, but not much more. Most of us are poor at reading body language when asked to do it consciously. So if you ask a group of volunteers to decide if a person is lying, the group consciously starts to evaluate the body language. People in this situation tend to fall back on remembered bits of lore, most of it inaccurate, rather than relying on their true expertise, which they can't access consciously precisely because it is unconscious. All of the studies show that they don't do better than mere chance. Even slices of the population that are supposed to be expert, such as police and FBI agents, don't do much better than chance on a consistent basis.[4]

So the hands and arms can indicate openness when they reach toward the other person and don't cross or fold protectively in front of the torso in some way. They indicate the opposite when they act protectively, either as crossed arms, or folded hands, or hands in the "fig leaf" position, or the like.

These kinds of mostly unconscious gestures are hard for most people to control because they originate in the deeper parts of the brain, before conscious thought. They are expressions of feelings, of emotion, of impressions of safety and danger, warmth and coldness, closeness and distance, open and closed. Most of us move our hands and arms in a constant ballet of unconscious gestures that both express and regulate how we are feeling about the place we are in, the people we are with, and the emotions we are experiencing.

READING NONVERBAL COMMUNICATION

We pick up constant readings on the emotional states of others, unconsciously as I've said, and to make them conscious would be to slow them down. But it would permit conscious response if we could also monitor our own behavior without slowing it down too much.

That's the challenge of nonverbal communication. We've evolved an exquisitely fine-tuned expertise in reading the intent of people around us, especially people we know well. We tend to stereotype strangers because we don't have the kind of detailed information that we do with people known to us. This expertise is unconscious, because it links at that level with our responses, our own gestures, and our own regulation of our safety and comfort. That means that we read only the simplest intentions (toward us) into the body language of strangers.

We don't make many allowances for others' behavior; we assume that they intend the most obvious actions that their nonverbal communications might possibly reveal. We read defensive or self-protective behavior as basically unfriendly; we tend not to assume that someone is merely shy. Similarly, we read aggressive behavior as just dangerous; we don't often assume it stems from insecurity.

Ironically, we tend to blame our own moments of clumsiness on extrinsic reasons—on being tired, having a bad day, or worrying about finances—whereas we blame others' behavior on their characters and intent: *he's just a robot; she's always cold like that; he's not a very fun guy, is he?*

I often work with people who resist having to change their behavior because they insist that they don't mean to be unfriendly, look nervous, or be closed off from an audience or colleagues, for example. It sometimes takes a good deal of persuasion for them to see that it's others' reading of their intentions that matter, not what the client may actually mean by his or her behavior.

CHANGING NONVERBAL BEHAVIOR

My partner and I worked with an executive of a major financial institution who had fought his way up from the streets, literally, to an executive position. When we were brought in to work with him, he had been promoted to a board-level position, and that required that he act in a statesmanlike manner, collegial, above the fray, and a mentor to others.

He had no idea how to behave in this way. All of his experience had taught him that he had to fight to keep his position and that colleagues were competition—even enemies sometimes. So when he went into a meeting with the board, he evinced the same behavior that he always had. And he was close to being fired.

We quickly discovered what it was that so turned off the board when we had him role-play his executive meetings. He would go into an ever-so-slight defensive crouch, unconsciously hunkering down like a football player getting ready for the hike, tensing himself, guarding himself with his arms and hands, and lowering his brows in a suspicious stare that had successfully intimidated many rivals in his earlier days.

He was completely unaware of this closed behavior. It was so much a part of his life, and had been for so long, that it was unconscious. He had been aware of his reputation as a tough in-fighter but had done nothing to discourage that, figuring that it would help him in the corporate wars. And it had—up to a point. Or rather, he had succeeded in spite of the closed behavior and because he was so good at his job. As a colleague, he had been endured rather than liked.

The 360-degree review he had received just after taking the new position had shocked him. He had no idea that people saw him as such a nasty guy. He felt that he did what he had to do to survive, precisely as he had on the streets as a boy. But now he realized that he had to learn a different way to relate to his colleagues. The board had no wish to spar continuously with a defensive, hostile executive; they wanted a colleague. Their comments and the review made it clear that he had to change.

He wasn't happy about it. The executive complained to us that he had been sent to us to "make nice." He thought that was our job: to help him learn to be a pushover or a hypocrite—someone who smiled a lot and pretended to be everyone's pal. So he was resistant. He recognized that people thought he was mean, but he didn't feel mean, and he resented having to change.

When we showed him the videotape of his role play, though, the moment was transformational. He had had no idea that his body language was signaling defensiveness. His reaction was, "Oh, my god, I look like a punk!" He knew that he couldn't look like a punk and continue as a C-suite executive.

That ten-minute video review probably saved his career. It gave him the motivation to change, and he slowly but surely learned to open up and thus become more of a colleague, and with the same tenacity that he had learned his street fighting.

In his case, it worked best for him to first monitor his behavior and then slowly work on changing it. He adopted a new posture and began to sit up straighter. Gradually he was able to open up his hands and arms. All of this took time and conscious effort before the new behavior became as comfortable and automatic as the old.

CREATING A NEW PERSONA THROUGH COMMUNICATION

When you communicate, you create a persona, one that you are only partly aware of, and it is that persona whose nonverbal signals of intentions other people unconsciously decode to determine how they should respond to you. The point of this book is to help leaders become fully aware of that persona so that they can control their communications and send out only the messages they wish. As should be clear by now, to do that successfully requires mastering the two conversations: the verbal (the content) and the nonverbal (the body language).

There is risk in making your persona and its body language conscious. Since body language originates in the pre-conscious part of the brain, in response to its rapid reading of the environment and its threats and opportunities, making it conscious will slow your gestures and your responsiveness. If that happens, you will get your speaking and gesturing out of sync, and people will unconsciously read your behavior as forced, fake, robotic, unnatural, or the like.

So how do you overcome this paradox of needing to control your two conversations to become an effective, persuasive, authentic communicator and yet gaining control can mean that you will be perceived as ineffective, unpersuasive, and inauthentic? You need another way to regulate body language—one that doesn't involve constant, conscious regulation of gesture and all the other aspects of body language that people read.

Fortunately, another way is at hand. If instead of working on the conscious control of body language, you work instead on the conscious control of intention, you will find that the gestures take care of themselves.

As I said in Chapter Two, this approach is akin to what actors do in method acting, after Constantin Stanislavski, the Russian actor and director who developed a systematic approach to the theater that focused on efforts to root acting in naturalistic behavior. The approach in the United States has come to mean almost exclusively working from emotional memories—to act sad by recalling a time when you really were sad—but Stanislavski himself took a much more holistic approach. The point was to find ways to achieve naturalistic effects whatever the source of those effects.

What I've found working with clients is that most people have great difficulty in devoting enough brain power to controlling the second conversation consciously. They're busy conversing, or speaking, or meeting, or having dinner, or doing whatever else it is they're supposed to be doing. Precisely because nonverbal behavior is predominantly unconscious, to make it conscious and then control it requires great effort.

Some highly advanced speakers already have enough self-awareness so that controlling their motion, say, or their hand gestures doesn't require much additional effort. But for most people, it's a slow process, and one replete with lots of back-sliding, to gain complete, conscious control over one's gestures. And to make those gestures look unstudied requires additional effort.

I worked with a well-known motivational speaker who both preached and believed that it wasn't talent that got her to where she was but hard work. She sent me the DVD of one speech early in our working relationship. At our next meeting, we spent five hours dissecting her verbal and nonverbal behavior in this forty-five-minute speech as we went through the DVD virtually frame by frame.

But few people have that much discipline or patience, so I searched for a better way to coach people to become authentic, persuasive, charismatic communicators. How could we break authenticity and charisma down into easily manageable activities that one could learn without all the conscious effort required of people who want to control their body language?

After many years of watching what works when we're communicating, I found the first piece easy to determine. In the broadest sense, most of the nonverbal mistakes that speakers, people in meetings, and those in conversation make stem from not being open to the others. Because of nervousness, evasiveness, attempts at deception, shyness, mixed emotions, and so on, people fail to be open to one another. And the result is that no powerful persuasive communication can take place. If that door is not open between people, no one passes through.

What happens when there's a mismatch—when one party to the communication is open and the other is closed? Then there is enormous pressure for the two of them to reach an accommodation. Either the closed one opens up, or the open one shuts down. It takes large disagreements or real emotional disconnections for the imbalance to persist. Usually the open person gives up if no progress is made. So the goal is to be open, as a first step, without thinking too hard about body language at all, because if you do (making your nonverbal actions conscious, in other words) you will slow it down to the point that it will unconsciously affect the people you're communicating with.

To accomplish this paradoxical feat, you simply think about someone with whom you would be delighted to be open. You think about your spouse, your child, or a friend. You imagine that you're about to see that person after a long absence and you're delighted to be together. In other words, you role-play in your mind a communication between you and your favorite person. Of course, if you have a tortured relationship with that favorite person, this won't help. You'll role-play those mixed messages. So pick someone with whom your relationship is easy, comfortable, close, and positive.

The better you are at imagining the situation and the other person, the more convincing you're going to be. If you think you're not any good at pretending, then simply notice your behavior the next time you are with that person (the one it's easy to be open with). Form a memory of what that feels like physically, not about what you say. Notice everything you can about your behavior. What are your facial gestures? Where is your face in relation to the other person? What are you doing with your hands? How is your torso positioned? How close are you? Are you touching each other? If so, what parts of your bodies are touching? And so on. Catalogue and remember the behavior, and then use that behavior when you're in a crucial meeting.

The results, if you do this faithfully, will surprise you. You will find yourself opening up to the people in the room and to the situation, and saying things that are more open than you otherwise might. That's because gestures precede thought, and your conscious mind is matching up with your open non-verbal behavior by being more open.

I have seen this behavior over and over again in the past couple of years as I have worked with people on openness. Working either from the inside out (forming the intent to be open by thinking about communicating with a loved one) or the outside in (simply standing with open arms, for example) helps people to open up verbally. The former way works better for most people because it looks more natural and usually has the benefit of injecting enthusiasm and energy into the occasion (most people are happy to imagine talking to that loved one).

Once you've tried this open behavior, remember it as best you can. The goal is to create a sense memory, as actors say, of what it feels like to be open. Practice will help you jump into that open state faster and faster, and more and more easily.

It's important to stay at the level of feeling. If you try to intellectualize the process too much or think about a specific gesture, you'll get the gesture wrong or too late. More important, you'll miss out on all the other tiny adjustments to behavior that continually register our state of mind to the others in the room and are just as continually recorded (and responded to) by the others. Most of this behavior is unconscious.

Practice this behavior in all sorts of appropriate situations. If, for example, you are walking through an airport terminal, being open all the way, with your posture tall, your head held high, your eyes open, smiling, and walking with energy, you'll be amazed at the result. People will make way for you, assuming you are a VIP. You may even get upgraded if you approach the counter confidently enough! No guarantees, but it's worth a try.

I'm cheating a little here, because I'm asking you to throw some confidence in with the openness to achieve the desired result of VIP status. To achieve that requires a shift in posture too. Again, you can achieve this by thinking about your intent to be confident. Remember a time when you were incredibly confident, or had just won a prize, or were on top of the world for some other reason. Then recall the physical behavior that went with it. Confident people stand tall, shoulders back, stomach in, and head up—like a soldier but without the tension. It is possible to be open without being confident, but I don't recommend it for leaders.

The point is to practice openness and confidence in a variety of situations and kinds of communication. The position you're in will affect your degree of openness in surprising ways. Sitting in an overstuffed chair around a big boardroom table, for example, means that most of you is hidden from everyone else. This does not encourage openness and may account for a good deal of the shenanigans that go on in boardrooms around the world.

If the goal in that situation is to be open, then you will find it better to stand and work the room, getting into the personal space of a number of people around the table, in order to have a powerful effect on all those half-hidden people.

AN EXAMPLE

It is impossible to catalogue all the small variations in gesture that signal degrees of openness. And by now you should realize that it works against what we're trying to accomplish to focus on specific gestures consciously. So I won't try to describe all the ways in which you could have the intent to be open and yet not be open enough.

I'll give an example, one that we see in our work with clients all the time. They typically know that they can't cross their arms in front of themselves in the classic defensive posture. So instead they pin their arms to their sides and just move their hands from the elbow down in front of themselves. I call it the penguin gesture, and it's a form of defensiveness.

Try it, and you'll see what I mean. Stand up, put your arms close to your sides, and then wave your hands in front of your stomach moving them only from the elbow down. That's the penguin gesture. It's defensive, and it's never open. It's more open than crossing your arms completely, but it's still partially closed.

Someone who is doing that gesture is feeling only partly open. So if you see yourself using the penguin gesture, try to strengthen your intent to be open. Pick a different favorite person, or ratchet up the intensity of feeling in some way. Probably that will bring you the openness you need.

The point here is that you should focus on the emotional state of openness and then see what the physical results are, because the gestures you use should then be appropriate for you and the situation. Once you get used to inhabiting your own skin when you're being open, you can note the details of what your body is doing and start to use that physical memory to help you get back into the right emotional state of openness. With practice, it gets easier and easier.

Openness in communication, especially in nonverbal communication, is the first step toward creating authenticity and charisma as a leader. Without it, you can't begin to connect with your audiences. With openness, the rest of the steps are possible, and you can become an effective communicator.

Being Connected, Part One

How to Master the Verbal Connection

The second step in the four-step layered process of communicating authentically is to connect with the audience. We all know that the industrialized world is awash in information today; many have observed that this information overload puts a heavy burden on would-be communicators to get the attention of their audiences. Whether it's a distracted spouse, a teenager playing a video game, a team worried about impending layoffs, a board that finds your report on sales initiatives tedious, an audience that's looking forward to lunch, or a press corps that's heard it all before, grabbing people in order to communicate with them has become a tall order. That means the process of connection is difficult and fraught with opportunities to lose, and yet it is more essential than ever before.

There are both verbal and nonverbal strategies to connecting with an audience, and powerfully, every time. I'll start with the verbal in this chapter.

FOCUS ON THE AUDIENCE'S CONCERNS

Connected communication deals with the audience's concerns. If people are overwhelmed with too much information, they respond by filtering in several ways. *People listen to ideas that are new, surprising, or world altering within their own frame of reference.* In other words, if you want to tell the world about your better mousetrap, the first group of people who are going to be interested are the folks who are plagued with mice. Those who are more worried about insects will give you a pass. If your idea turns out not to be different in any way, you'll quickly lose the interest of your audience; they will begin to filter you out. In order to keep from being overwhelmed by information, we filter by novelty, but only in the areas that we have decided we care about.

People listen to ideas from trusted sources. Another way in which we filter is to cut down on the number of sources we will listen to. This makes communicating with new audiences particularly challenging. Why should they pay attention to you? They already have their go-to people identified. One relative is good on cars, a sister is good on fashion, someone at work knows the powers that be, and so on. It's hard to crack into that lineup if you're not proven. To become a trusted source mostly takes time and an introduction from an already trusted source. It's the Tupperware party effect: we get an invitation from a friend, and once we're in the door, our resistance drops. But we never would have gone if someone we knew hadn't invited us.

People listen to ideas from sources that are (objectively) well known or often available to them. Another way we vet ideas is to consider the reputation of the source if it isn't a trusted one already. And here we use conventional means: we judge the level of authority, celebrity, or even notoriety by all the usual measures. It often takes frequent repetition of the message from the source for us to finally hear it if it is not already trusted.

We all have different ideas of objective sources, but the differences usually aren't particularly wide or surprising. You may like to get your new from CBS; I may prefer the *Financial Times* or the BBC. Oprah may be your source for new book recommendations; I may read the *New York Times Book Review*. Only relatively small numbers of people go to fringe sources for this kind of information.

Expertise is another matter. Generally the more you know about a particular field of inquiry, the more specialized your sources are. You are far more likely to distrust the standard sources if you have deep knowledge of a subject.

People listen to ideas that fulfill a deep need. If our need seems great enough, we'll break every other rule in order to find a solution, even turning to ideas that seem outré to us and sources that we have not completely vetted. In Chapter Twelve, where I go into a great deal of detail and background for those who want the full story, I use Abraham Maslow's hierarchy of needs to help make this clear. If we're trying to satisfy needs that are way down the hierarchy (like safety), then we'll be more likely to listen to solutions that respond to that level of need for us. And we'll be more open to solutions generally because deep needs are felt more urgently than the higher ones like self-actualization in Maslow's terms.

When my aunt was dying of cancer, she and my uncle turned to all kinds of risky cancer treatment programs, even going to Mexico at one point for what can only be described as a charlatan. They eagerly scanned the medical news and every source they could think of for hope, new options, and experimental treatments. It was a tragic but understandable response to a desperate need.

USE LANGUAGE FAMILIAR TO THE AUDIENCE

Connected communication is phrased in the audience's own language. This is a simple point, but one that many forget. Insider language, jargon, identification with those you're communicating with: all of these can strengthen the connection if they are used to highlight the bond between you. Of course, if the jargon gets in the way of communication or sounds forced or fake, it won't work. But used as a gesture of solidarity, it can have great impact.

A classic example of this phenomenon is President Kennedy's "Ich bin ein Berliner" speech on June 26, 1963, in Berlin. The speech sought to express solidarity with the citizens of Berlin, surrounded by East Germany and feeling isolated during some of the darkest years of the cold war. By using the German phrase, Kennedy said he was one of them, both literally and emotionally. The crowd went wild, and riots broke out. Truly, this was a world-changing speech. It didn't even matter that *Ich bin ein Berliner* means, "I am a jelly doughnut," since a *berliner* is a popular pastry. The audience got the idea even though Kennedy's German was imperfect.[1]

BE DIRECT AND SIMPLE

Connected communication is direct and simple. Communication that cuts through the usual clutter, euphemisms, and verbiage can be powerfully effective. When you start with a truth that hasn't been uttered out loud before, you get people's attention. We're so used to being sold in today's marketing-saturated world that simple language about real concerns can cut through the noise.

If you really want to get people's attention, tell them a direct truth that no one else is speaking aloud. *Sexual Behavior in the Human Male*, the first of the so-called Kinsey Reports, published in 1948, and its companion volume, *Sexual Behavior in the Human Female*, published in 1953, grabbed enormous attention, positive and negative, because of their frankness about a topic that had hitherto not been much discussed in public.[2]

On another level, Prime Minister Winston Churchill's simple, direct language in his speeches accounts for a good deal of their powerful impact. Here is one of his famous utterances in the House of Commons on May 13, 1940, when he became prime minister in very dark times for England indeed:

> I would say to the House, as I said to those who have
> joined the Government: "I have nothing to offer
> but blood, toil, tears and sweat."
> We have before us an ordeal of the most grievous
> kind. We have before us many, many long months
> of struggle and of suffering. You ask, what is our policy?
> I will say: It is to wage war, by sea, land and air, with

all our might and with all the strength that God can give us: to wage war against a monstrous tyranny, never surpassed in the dark, lamentable catalogue of human crime. That is our policy. You ask, What is our aim? I can answer in one word: Victory—victory at all costs, victory in spite of all terror, victory, however long and hard the road may be: for without victory, there is no survival. Let that be realized; no survival for the British Empire; no survival for all that the British Empire has stood for, no survival for the urge and impulse of the ages, that mankind will move forward towards its goal. But I take up my task with buoyancy and hope. I feel sure that our cause will not be suffered to fail among men. At this time I feel entitled to claim the aid of all, and I say, "Come, then, let us go forward together with our united strength."[3]

Churchill's rhetoric was powerful because it was straightforward. He used clear words to label his vision of the good and evil in the contest—*monstrous tyranny, never surpassed in the dark, lamentable catalogue of human crime*—leaving no one in any doubt where he stood. And the simple question-and-answer format allowed him to state his goal in unequivocal terms: "Victory—victory at all costs, victory in spite of all terror, victory, however long and hard the road may be: for without victory, there is no survival." It is no exaggeration to say that a good deal of Churchill's power as a leader came from his willingness to use simple words to express his thoughts powerfully and directly to wide audiences.

USE *YOU* AND *WE*

Connected communication uses *you* and *we* more than *I*, a simple point that is often forgotten. People like to hear about themselves, and, with rare exceptions, they like having the focus on them. Your language is a tip-off as to how well you're accomplishing that. If you're using the word *I* a great deal, you're not communicating; you're soliloquizing.

Compare a brief excerpt from former President Bill Clinton's memoir, *My Life*, with one from a well-known political reporter. Here's Clinton:

> When I was in high school, I played the tenor saxophone solo on a piece about New Orleans called Crescent City Suite. I always thought I did a better job on it because I played it with memories of my first sight of the city. When I was twenty-one, I won a Rhodes scholarship in New Orleans. I think I did well in the interview in part because I felt at home there. When I was a young law professor, Hillary and I had a couple of great trips to New Orleans for conventions, staying at a quaint little hotel in the French Quarter, the Cornstalk.[4]

Clinton used *I* twelve times in just over five sentences.

This is the excerpt from Jack Germond, veteran reporter and author of *Fat Man in a Middle Seat*, writing about his life as a young man:

> Working for *The Evening News* [his first job out of college] was an almost entirely misleading experience. The owner and publisher of the paper, JS Gray, no

periods after the initials—belonged in a newspaper textbook. He was totally professional and so was his newspaper, not in the sense that it was a polished and sophisticated product but in the sense that it understood its place in the community. It was there to print the news, no more and no less. There was no boosterism, no political agenda, no favorites to be coddled. JS backed his reporters to the hilt.[5]

In six sentences, Germond didn't use *I* a single time. Of course, I could pick other passages where Jack does talk about himself, but both of these selections are random and typical.

It is reasonable to conclude that former President Clinton is a good deal more self-absorbed than Jack Germond— perhaps with justification but nonetheless more self-absorbed. Both men, to be sure, are writing memoirs, so they're supposed to be talking about themselves, but one of them makes the story about himself, and the other makes it about the people in his life. Neither addressed the audience as much as truly connected conversation does. Look again at the excerpt from Churchill's speech and you'll see a certain number of *I*'s, but also *you, we,* and *us.* It's a profoundly connected communication.

REMEMBER THAT COMMUNICATION IS RECIPROCAL

Connected communication is reciprocal. For the most part, people feel obligated to listen if you've listened to them. Some self-absorbed people never reciprocate, but most of us do because the golden rule is deeply baked into our psyches.

So a good way to begin a communication is to find out what the other person (or group) has on its mind.[6]

A classic mistake that many consultants make when they're meeting a client for the first time, in either informal settings or more formal presentations, is to begin "by introducing ourselves." The first ten minutes or so of the discussion is all about them. Nothing could be less engaging for the potential client. Why should she care?

A much better way is to begin by showing that you understand the client's problems. Even better is to get the client to tell you her problem. Either way is more connecting and involving than the self-introduction. When my partner and I work with consultants preparing for a client meeting, we almost always have to tell them to remove the lengthy discussion of the firm's credentials, or at least save it until later, when the client's interest has been clearly established.

BE CONSISTENT

Connected communication is consistent. We don't like to experience ourselves as inconsistent, so if I can snare your attention once, I'm likely to be able to get it again unless I've abused the privilege.[7] People prefer the familiar to the strange in most things. It's why clichés are clichés, after all. Why go to all the work of developing a new source or finding a new expert if the old one will do?

Once a celebrity, a newscaster, or a politician reaches the top of the heap, the sheer inertia of their audiences will keep them there until they do something egregious enough to warrant pushing them out and finding a replacement.

PAY ATTENTION TO THE SOCIAL ASPECT

Connected communication is social. If everyone's doing it, we're more likely to join in unless we have an oppositional streak. Communications success breeds communications success.[8] This explains fads and the popularity of otherwise inexplicable things (like Barry Manilow).

Malcolm Gladwell has explored this aspect of communication thoroughly in *The Tipping Point*. He argues that a combination of people who are naturally more gregarious than the rest of us and the theory that ideas spread like infectious diseases adds up to a moment when suddenly everyone is aware of a new idea, phenomenon, or fad. I add that part of Gladwell's success surely stems from the fact that his idea is relatively simple and yet recognizable. We all understand intuitively how fads are unknown except to a few at one moment and then ubiquitous at the next. Once again, we prefer the familiar to the recondite and strange.[9]

USE THE CALL OF YOUR OWN TRIBE

We connect better with people who are like us. Again, this is a simple rule that is often forgotten. In a world awash with information, especially if we feel threatened or disoriented by that overload of new data, we tend to go tribal and safe and cluster with people most like ourselves. Similarly, we are likely to recognize first the things that are most familiar to us: ourselves and the habits and activities we always engage in.[10] The call of our own tribe is very powerful for us; it explains the lasting popularity of clubs, fraternities and sororities, secret societies, and all the other ways people employ to include some and exclude others.

Churchill passionately invoked this rule of connected communication in one of his most famous speeches, given to the House of Commons on June 18, 1940:

> What General Weygand called the Battle of France
> is over. I expect that the Battle of Britain is about to
> begin. Upon this battle depends the survival of Christian
> civilization. Upon it depends our own British life, and
> the long continuity of our institutions and our Empire.
> The whole fury and might of the enemy must very soon
> be turned on us. Hitler knows that he will have to break
> us in this island or lose the war. If we can stand up to
> him, all Europe may be free and the life of the world
> may move forward into broad, sunlit uplands. But if we
> fail, then the whole world, including the United States,
> including all that we have known and cared for, will sink
> into the abyss of a new Dark Age made more sinister,
> and perhaps more protracted, by the lights of perverted
> science. Let us therefore brace ourselves to our duties
> and so bear ourselves that, if the British Empire and its
> Commonwealth last for a thousand years, men will still
> say, "This was their finest hour."[11]

This is a tribal call to arms at its most eloquent. Of course, on the other side, Hitler was making parallel calls to what he termed the "Aryan race" no less passionately and no less effectively in the short run. All of World War II is in that sense a macabre testimony to the power of our urge to connect with people like us and, by extension, exclude people not like us.

EMBRACE THE NEW

Finally, and paradoxically, we also connect better with ideas, communications, and people whom we perceive to be unusual, scarce, or rare.[12] We are perverse creatures and can one day ignore and the next day embrace an idea, a communication, or a person who is unusual to us. Indeed, an opposing and equally powerful human urge, in opposition to the tribal instinct, is to take the stranger in and make him or her familiar. The collector's desire for the stamp, or the painting, or the snuff box that no one else has is akin to this aspect of communication. When we feel safe enough to do so, we will embrace the new, the odd, or the truly weird—but only when we feel safe.

The adventuresome among us—Gladwell calls them "collectors, mavens, and salesmen"—bring us these new and strange ideas and are responsible for making them achieve fad status or widespread adoption.[13] This kind of receptivity, though, is limited to a small percentage of the population most of the time and more of us at certain times. When we feel prosperous, magnanimous, or safe as a population, we are better able to look beyond our immediate concerns and entertain a broader array of communication possibilities.

As soon as the economy or the social climate turns scary, though, we're back to the familiar and the trusted source. Communication success depends very much on how it's pitched and when it is being put forward.

6

Being Connected, Part Two

How to Master the Nonverbal Connection

W hat about the nonverbal ways people can get connected? Once again, I'll first explore what the research and my experience show and then give a holistic means for putting it together, along with openness, to achieve an authentic relationship with your audience, whether it's one person or one thousand.

CONNECTION IS CLOSENESS

Not surprisingly, perhaps, connection is first and foremost about closeness.[1] We all unconsciously measure the distance between ourselves and everyone else for obvious reasons of self-protection first and interest second. Twelve feet or more is public space, the coolest connection between people. Between twelve feet and four feet is social space, a little warmer than public space but still cool. Four feet to a foot and a half is personal space, and now things are beginning to get interesting for us. A foot and a half to zero is intimate space, and we let only people we trust highly or are very fond of in this space. These spaces vary a bit from culture to culture; Mediterranean and Asian cultures tend to shrink the distances, and Western cultures preserve them. But all of us have the four zones.

Try them out yourself. Walk down the street in a small town, and note when you make eye contact with approaching strangers and when they make eye contact with you. You will find that it is always close to twelve feet. I assume this is because at that distance, we can still do something about a danger that presents itself; any closer and we might not have time to react.

Now try the move into the personal zone with someone. You'll see that you keep your eyes, at minimum, on each other, and usually you'll change your entire physical orientation when someone moves into your personal space. Interest and energy increase. Your heart rate increases slightly. It's personal, and you're connected.

If you move into someone's intimate space, a new level of tension arises, unless of course you are already intimate with that person—a spouse, a very close friend, a parent, or a child. If you're not intimate, the closeness will feel uncomfortable for both of you, and typically one or the other of the two people will try to draw back into safer personal space.

I've demonstrated this phenomenon many times to audiences I've lectured to about communication, and it usually gets a laugh because of the discomfort everyone feels.

Once I was talking about the zones with a small group of executives, and I moved into the intimate space of one of the women in the room as I was talking. She responded by giving me a solid right hook to the chest! She apologized afterward, but of course she was simply responding with instinctive appropriateness because I had violated her intimate zone. Once we all recovered, this incident made the point very well to everyone in the room about how important it is to understand the four zones and how deeply people are conditioned to maintain them. No doubt they developed in prehistoric times as a matter of life and death.

We've all seen drill sergeants in movies who put their face an inch or two from the hapless inductee and say in stentorian tones that he's a maggot. The point here is that the inductee is not allowed to maintain his intimate space; he's being broken down in order to be built up again as a Marine, for example. Partly it's just good theater, but it also violates a real sense of self-protection and so is destabilizing and humiliating for the inductee. These zones are powerful reminders that we are animals who carefully guard our physical and psychic integrity and protect ourselves unconsciously at all times.

HOW TO USE SOCIAL AND INTIMATE SPACE

So how do you use these zones to increase the connectedness with the person or persons you're trying to communicate with? Everything significant in communication between people happens in personal space or intimate space. That's the most important thing to remember about connection. There has been a historical change in this regard with the advent of television. What was once social or public now is personal.

In other words, seeing newscasters, celebrities, and politicians in our living rooms and bedrooms for all these years has created an expectation that we can have personal conversations with everyone who matters to us. The head-and-shoulders framing of people on TV gives the appearance of that personal space closeness to us, and we've gotten used to it.

Your goal as a communicator is to make sure of a couple of things. First, you're in the personal space of the person you're communicating with when you're saying the most important things, asking for what you really want, or closing the sale. Second, whenever you're attempting to communicate with someone, you're closing the distance between you rather than increasing it.

I see people move away from audiences all the time when they're giving a speech for reasons of nerves, or self-protection, or something else. The result is that the second conversation says to the audience, "This is not important; you don't need to pay attention," even while the poor speaker is trying to make some point he or she believes *is* important. The two conversations are not supporting one another, and the audience believes the second every time.

So to connect nonverbally, you need to move toward people and use the four zones of space to make it personal. When you want to cool the relationship down or punctuate your communication, say, by signaling that you're changing the subject, you can move away at that point. That move will demonstrate more eloquently than anything you can say that a change has happened.

Is that really all there is to it? Not quite. You can increase the connection with people by making eye contact and using facial gestures, most notably raised eyebrows, to ask for a response.

SIGNAL YOUR INTENT WITH YOUR POSTURE

You can also signal your intent with your posture. Remember that people are unconsciously sizing you up all the time: reading your intent and figuring out important things like whether you are friend or foe. They derive a huge part of that intent from your posture.

Once again, this is something that I've demonstrated many times to audiences in talks on communications. You can try it yourself. Begin by noticing how people stand from the side, as if you were cutting a two-dimensional slice from top to bottom. You'll see that people stand in one of three ways primarily. There's a fourth, but it's rare, and a combination of two of the others.

First, some people stand with their head leading, keeping it forward from the perpendicular. We read this posture as submissive, intellectual, uncertain, or deferential. Try it yourself by standing up straight, at attention, like a soldier. Imagine that a string tied to the top of your head is pulling it up as high and straight as it will go. Then pitch your head forward and round your shoulders as you do so. That's the head posture. You will notice that you begin to feel submissive, deferential, and uncertain if you adopt this posture near someone else.

The second posture leads with the pelvis. Rock stars and teenagers adopt this posture all the time. Begin in the upright posture again, and then pitch your pelvis forward (it may help to play a little air guitar at the same time). This posture is highly sexual and will provoke a sexual reaction in the people you communicate with in this way.

I once worked with a high-powered consultant who had recently been promoted within her firm to take on the most important clients. She had a series of boardroom meetings with big companies, and they did not go well. I was called in to advise her, and we role-played the meetings. It became instantly clear why she was not commanding the respect of the boards she was dealing with: she was standing in a highly pelvic posture. The result was that the board was seeing her as a sexual object, not a high-powered consultant. Interestingly, she was completely unaware of her posture. I videotaped her performance, and she could instantly see what was wrong. She changed her posture, and her consulting work improved immediately. Sometimes solutions are simple.

The third, and best, posture if you're trying to communicate authentically with people and build their trust is the heart posture. Adopting the upright posture again, with your head held high (imagining the string once more). Now throw your shoulders back even a little more, but try not to make them tense with the effort and don't raise them up. Relax your shoulders down and back, and keep your head and neck high. Roll the small of your back forward, and tuck your stomach in.

That's the heart posture, and it is the one that trustworthy people adopt unconsciously and the one that other people trust. If you use this posture, people more easily connect with you. They will be inclined to open up to you and let you in.

That's how you make connection possible with them. Posture and distance—or, rather, nearness.

The fourth posture is a combination of the first two: a pushed forward head and pelvis. It's the posture of a self-conscious, sexualized teenager or an intellectual rocker. Don't try it at home or anywhere else.

NOW CREATE THE INTENT TO BE CONNECTED

How do you achieve all this without constantly monitoring your posture and the distance between yourself and others? Once again, if you create the intent to be connected with people, the rest will follow.

Here's the way to think about it. If you have or have had teenage children, this exercise will be particularly easy for you. Imagine that you have something important to tell someone you love. Perhaps you've just had some great news, and you're itching to tell your teenage daughter. You knock on her door, and over the roar of some unidentifiable (and horrible) music, you dimly hear, "Yeah?" from the other side of the door. You steel yourself and walk in. There she is, slouched in her chair, IM-ing someone about homework, texting her friends about something (you have no idea), and listening to MegaDeath.

How do you get her attention? You move closer probably, raise your voice perhaps, and gesticulate almost certainly; you somehow cut through all her various distractions to make sure that she hears you. You make eye contact, and you may even grab her elbow or tap her on the shoulder. Think about what you do when it is absolutely essential that she hear you. Your intent is clear and strong; you will not be denied. You absolutely mean it! This is not a case of nice-to-have; it's must-have. It's a combination of a number of things: physical proximity, tone of voice, posture, and gesture, among others.

That's connection. Keep that image of the distracted teenager firmly fixed in your mind, and you will achieve connection. Of course, you must connect politely, tactfully, and appropriately. But use all the energy you need to do so. Most people fail at communications for lack of energy, signaling an uncommitted second conversation. So the other person doesn't believe you mean it and doesn't pay attention.

Once again, keep your efforts at the level of intent. Try not to become consciously aware of, say, your eye contact or your gestures when you are trying to connect. They will look studied and artificial if you will them to happen. If you simply intend to connect, it will go better, and look authentic.

I remember collapsing in laughter once long ago when I was traveling abroad with my parents, watching my mother attempt to communicate with a supercilious French waiter by talking VERY LOUDLY AND V-E-R-Y S-L-O-W-L-Y. I thought it was the funniest, dumbest attempt I'd ever seen, obviously doomed to failure. But she was using the instinctive tools at her command to make a connection. And her effort worked, to a point. The French waiter talked back at her, raising his connection ante just as she did. Only he gesticulated more and more animatedly, using all his Gallic tools to make a connection and persuade the irritating American woman not to have her omelet overcooked. Those instincts are powerful, and when they are working for you, they will help you connect authentically with your audience, however large it is.

Openness and connection are the essential steps to communicating authentically with an audience of one or one thousand. These first two steps govern authenticity in the main; the following two will help you become charismatic.

How to Be Passionate with Content

The third step in the layered process of communicating authentically and charismatically is being passionate—showing your heart. It's the reason, in the end, that you communicate, and it's where charisma begins to enter the picture in a meaningful way. It's the opportunity we all crave to know and be known by someone else. It's the only meaningful evidence, in the long run, that we were ever alive on the planet. And it's the chance to form a bond that endures beyond the moment.

Why then is it step three if it's so important? Because your heart will be rebuffed by the person you're trying to communicate with if you haven't established openness and connection. You'd be like the crackpot stranger in the street who grabs someone's sleeve and says, "Hey, buddy, the world is coming to an end, and I know when!" Your first reaction is to think, *Who the hell is this?* because you're not open to each other. And your second reaction, if you get that far, is, *Why me?* Because you're not connected.

Showing your heart to someone is neither trivial nor easy. Trust must be firmly established, and the way to do that is through openness and connection.

Once again, being passionate has a verbal and a nonverbal component. We'll look at the verbal side first.

Given that passion obviously involves emotion, and emotion gives rise first to gesture, how do you effectively communicate passion through your content? Recognize that all the verbal expressions of emotion are not as strong as the nonverbal ones, and if the two are at odds, the person you're communicating with will believe the nonverbal always.

LABEL THE EMOTION

That said, there are some ways to express passion through content. The first, and simplest, technique is to label the emotion. And yet this technique is one that people deny themselves all the time, because of our reluctance to talk about negative or strong emotions. Is it easy to look at a loved one and say, "I'm angry with you"? How about going into your boss's office and saying, "Boss, I'm really frustrated because you have systematically underfunded and understaffed this initiative, and you know my career depends on its success"? And what about telling an old friend that he's let you down by not showing up at a performance that really mattered to you?

People go through years of therapy and read countless books on how to accomplish this simple yet powerful technique—all to overcome a societal taboo against expressing oneself. We are uncomfortable with negative emotions and worry that the expression of strong emotions will make us look out of control.

We should all get over it. At its most extreme, this reluctance to speak the truth can lead literally to violent death. More than one plane crash has occurred because the copilot has felt reluctant to criticize the misjudgments of the pilot, so entrenched is the chain of command on commercial airlines. The rest of us who are not airline pilots may not risk death, but we do endanger relationships and frustrate everyone when we hold back from telling the truth and just labeling the emotion.

Presidential candidate Barack Obama used this technique in a powerful speech he gave as a response to the publicity surrounding the angry words of his former pastor, the Reverend Jeremiah Wright. The result was to open a dialogue at a level of honesty that had not been heard since Martin Luther King Jr. was alive. The speech, given in Philadelphia on March 18, 2008, courageously labeled the emotions of both black and white Americans:

> But for all those who scratched and clawed their way
> to get a piece of the American Dream, there were
> many who didn't make it—those who were ultimately
> defeated, in one way or another, by discrimination. That
> legacy of defeat was passed on to future generations. . . .
> Even for those blacks who did make it, questions of
> race, and racism, continue to define their worldview in
> fundamental ways. For the men and women of Reverend
> Wright's generation, the memories of humiliation and
> doubt and fear have not gone away; nor has the anger
> and the bitterness of those years. That anger may not
> get expressed in public, in front of white co-workers or
> white friends. But it does find voice in the barbershop or
> around the kitchen table

And occasionally it finds voice in the church on Sunday morning, in the pulpit and in the pews. The fact that so many people are surprised to hear that anger in some of Reverend Wright's sermons simply reminds us of the old truism that the most segregated hour in American life occurs on Sunday morning. That anger is not always productive. . . . But the anger is real; it is powerful; and to simply wish it away, to condemn it without understanding its roots, only serves to widen the chasm of misunderstanding that exists between the races.

In fact, a similar anger exists within segments of the white community. Most working- and middle-class white Americans don't feel that they have been particularly privileged by their race. Their experience is the immigrant experience—as far as they're concerned, no one's handed them anything, they've built it from scratch. They've worked hard all their lives, many times only to see their jobs shipped overseas or their pension dumped after a lifetime of labor. They are anxious about their futures, and feel their dreams slipping away; in an era of stagnant wages and global competition, opportunity comes to be seen as a zero sum game, in which your dreams come at my expense. So when they are told to bus their children to a school across town; when they hear that an African-American is getting an advantage in landing a good job or a spot in a good college because of an injustice that they themselves never committed; when they're told that their fears about crime in urban neighborhoods are somehow prejudiced, resentment builds over time.[1]

This kind of rhetorical honesty puts the issue squarely in front of the audience. No evasion is possible after a speech like this. That's both the opportunity and the danger of labeling emotions. Once they're labeled, you have to deal with them if you have any integrity at all. And it's the same in more intimate conversations. Once a problem has been honestly and directly put in front of all parties, they must address it. This simple technique turns out to be surprisingly powerful.

TELL AN UNCOMFORTABLE TRUTH

Another equally simple yet profound technique to show passion in your verbal expression is to tell an uncomfortable truth. It's important to distinguish telling the truth from labeling the emotion. Certainly there can be overlap, but to tell an uncomfortable truth can often mean keeping your emotions in check. The passion that shows up in these instances is courage.

The classic instance of truth telling in this mode is whistle-blowing. From the cigarette industry to Enron, WorldCom, and the Federal Aviation Administration, whistle-blowers put their careers, their family's safety, and indeed their own lives on the line. Since the natural reaction of the institution that is being taken to task is to stonewall first and deny the credibility of the whistle-blower second, it is essential for the individual to appear not to be superficially emotional. We measure the power of their belief, ironically, by how much they appear to be holding back.

USE VERBAL RESTRAINT

We may generalize this technique to include many other instances when verbal restraint can be a more powerful indicator of depth of feeling than excess. When a parent gives a toast at a son or daughter's wedding, we get one kind of reading of how the parent feels if he or she weeps uncontrollably and another if instead we see someone who holds back the tears. The first performance is forgivable but vaguely embarrassing. The second is dignified, heart-wrenching, and an unforgettable way to demonstrate passion in verbal expression. Of course, the restraint in the verbal component has to be accompanied by a similar set of nonverbal cues of restraint with deep feeling behind the facade. Once again, we see how essential it is for the two conversations to be aligned for communication to be effective, authentic, and charismatic.

An amusing instance of this rule appears in the movie *Four Weddings and a Funeral*. Hugh Grant's character gives a marvelously funny toast in the first wedding, deftly suggesting all sorts of hilarious double entendres and potentially embarrassing recollections of the groom from his bachelor days. It is all very funny—because of the restraint: Hugh Grant never actually says anything directly. In a later wedding, one of his friends tries to do the same thing and ends up embarrassing himself, the bridal couple, and the assembled guests precisely because he doesn't know where to stop. Too much information kills the moment. A related technique is to focus on the physical details of a situation without labeling the emotions. This technique works when everyone knows that the situation is emotionally charged. Look at the perfectly realized, telling details from Norman Maclean's *A River Runs Through It* as the family struggles to cope with their wayward son's death from a savage beating over a gambling debt:

When I finished talking to my father, he asked, "Is there anything else you can tell me?"

Finally, I said, "Nearly all the bones in his hand were broken."

He almost reached the door and then turned back for reassurance. "Are you sure that the bones in his hand were broken?" he asked. I repeated, "Nearly all the bones in his hand were broken." "In which hand?" he asked. "In his right hand," I answered.

After my brother's death, my father never walked very well again. He had to struggle to lift his feet, and, when he did get them up, they came down slightly out of control. From time to time Paul's right hand had to be reaffirmed; then my father would shuffle away again.[2]

This scene is heartbreaking precisely because Maclean doesn't tell us what the father is feeling. We infer it from his shuffle and his need to have the damage to his son's right hand reaffirmed. Just as emotion can be powerful when it's labeled, it can also be powerful when it's hinted at in physical details that speak to it but do not directly label it.

How do you know when to use one technique and not the other? When the emotions are widely understood and shared, then restraint is more effective. When the emotions are not well understood or not widely shared, labeling them is more effective. Beyond that, tact in particular situations is essential.

A businessperson confronting the poor performance of a division needs to label his or her emotions so that no one is in doubt that there is a problem and it needs to be addressed.

In any case, there is so much withholding of emotions in the business world that being open about them is almost always powerful. There are exceptions: a boss who rules with fear and anger astonishes and captures the attention of no one when he lets loose with yet another outburst.

A politician talking about the loss of a hero should consider restraint. It's an unusual approach for a politician, to be sure, but all the more powerful because of that.

CONVEY EMOTION THROUGH RHETORIC

What other verbal techniques convey emotion? Oddly enough, perhaps, rhetorical elegance on more formal or important occasions can convey emotion when it isn't merely pompous. Two main techniques, the rhetorical rule of threes and (appropriate) repetition, are the most powerful ways to convey emotion through rhetoric.

Let's look at Martin Luther King Jr. giving what many believe was the most eloquent speech of the previous century at the Washington Mall on August 23, 1963.[3] First is the use of repetition to create passion:

> I say to you today, my friends, that in spite of the
> difficulties and frustrations of the moment I still have
> a dream. It is a dream deeply rooted in the American
> dream.
>
> I have a dream that one day this nation will rise up
> and live out the true meaning of its creed: "We hold
> these truths to be self-evident; that all men are created
> equal."

I have a dream that one day on the red hills of Georgia the sons of former slaves and the sons of former slave owners will be able to sit down together at the table of brotherhood.

I have a dream that one day even the state of Mississippi, a desert state sweltering in the heat of injustice and oppression, will be transformed into an oasis of freedom and justice.

I have a dream that my four little children will one day live in a nation where they will not be judged by the color of their skin but by the content of their character.

I have a dream today.

I have a dream that one day the state of Alabama, whose governor's lips are presently dripping with the words of interposition and nullification, will be transformed into a situation where little black boys and black girls will be able to join hands with little white boys and white girls and walk together as sisters and brothers.

I have a dream today.

There's a real art to repetition. How do you manage it so that it doesn't sound simple-minded but rather, as in this case, creates a crescendo of emotion that builds with each reaffirmation of the phrase, "I have a dream"? The key is the phrase that's repeated. It has to be able to bear the weight, and the words have to be affirmative, simple, and evocative. In King's case, the words were perfect. But it's not easy to find the right ones. The political world is full of repetitive phrasing and chanting of key phrases that the speaker begins and the audience takes over, but most of them are quickly forgotten.

The rule of three plays magnificently at the end of the speech, when King invokes a spiritual and brings the audience to its feet:

> When we let freedom ring, when we let it ring from every
> village and every hamlet, from every state and every city,
> we will be able to speed up that day when all of God's
> children, black men and white men, Jews and Gentiles,
> Protestants and Catholics, will be able to join hands and
> sing in the words of the old Negro spiritual, "Free at last!
> Free at last! Thank God Almighty, we are free at last!"

There are actually two sets of threes here: the group- ings of black and white, Jews and Gentiles, and Protestants and Catholics, as well as the final triumphant, "Free at last!" And there are further subtleties. By giving us two groups of two—*every village and every hamlet* and *every state and every city*—King creates in us a need to have the completion of a group of three. And of course he balances the two sets of groups perfectly. It's an amazing performance.

Perhaps you're thinking, *Well, that was easy for Reverend King. He was a great speaker and had time to prepare. But how can I achieve that kind of rhetorical passion in my communications, which are mostly off the cuff?* You may be astonished to find out that the second half of King's speech, where these quotes come from, was ad-libbed.

What is it about groups of three that heighten emotion and create passion? Why do we respond so powerfully to them? It's a mystery—something psychological. Some say it has to do with religious symbolism, since there are groups of three in most major religions, but that may be putting the cart before the horse: the religions may have settled on groups of threes for the same psychological reasons that everyone else finds them powerful. Whatever the reason, we find something complete and satisfying in a group of three, like a three-legged stool that can stand firmly on uneven ground, and thus you should use them in your communications when you're striving to convey passion.

USE TROPES AND METAPHORICAL DEVICES

Finally, the whole host of tropes and metaphorical devices bequeathed to us by the ancient Greeks can, when properly used, convey passion and stir emotion in the hearts of listeners.[4] Some of the more useful ones are rhetorical questions, metaphors and similes, of course, alliteration, antithesis, parallelism, synecdoche, personification, hyperbole, and irony.

· · ·

- *Rhetorical question.* A rhetorical question asserts a position rather than literally asking for an answer. In his inaugural address on January 20, 1961, President Kennedy asked, "Can we forge against these enemies a grand and global alliance, North and South, East and West, that can assure a more fruitful life for all mankind? Will you join in that historic effort?"[5] He was not literally asking his audience if that was possible. Rather, he asserted that that was what he wanted to do.
- *Metaphors and similes.* These compare one thing to another, a simile with *like* or *as* and the metaphor (the umbrella term) without it. In other words, one is explicit, the other implicit. *My love is like a red, red rose* is a simile. *My love is honey and balm* is a metaphor.

- *Alliteration*. Initial consonants or consonants in the middle of the word are repeated: *The last liberal living is an old lefty from Lebanon, Pennsylvania*.
- *Antithesis*. This device juxtaposes contrasting ideas, often with parallel structure. The most famous instance in the modern era comes again from Kennedy's inaugural address. Kennedy used antithesis throughout the speech, but most memorably at the end:

> In the long history of the world, only a few generations
> have been granted the role of defending freedom in
> its hour of maximum danger. I do not shrink from this
> responsibility—I welcome it. I do not believe that any of
> us would exchange places with any other people or any
> other generation. The energy, the faith, the devotion
> which we bring to this endeavor will light our country
> and all who serve it—and the glow from that fire can
> truly light the world.
>
> And so, my fellow Americans, ask not what your
> country can do for you—ask what you can do for your
> country.
>
> My fellow citizens of the world, ask not what
> America will do for you, but what together we can do for
> the freedom of man.

- *Parallelism*. Similar pairs or series of words, phrases, clauses, or sentences are used. A great example comes again from Kennedy's inaugural:

> This much we pledge—and more.

To those old allies whose cultural and spiritual origins we share, we pledge the loyalty of faithful friends. . . .

To those new states whom we welcome to the ranks of the free, we pledge our word that one form of colonial control shall not have passed away merely to be replaced by a far more iron tyranny. . . .

To those peoples in the huts and villages of half the globe struggling to break the bonds of mass misery, we pledge our best efforts to help them help themselves. . . .

To our sister republics south of our border we offer a special pledge—to convert our good words into good deeds—in a new alliance for progress to assist free men and free governments in casting off the chains of poverty. . . .

To that world assembly of sovereign states, the United Nations, our last best hope in an age where the instruments of war have far outpaced the instruments of peace, we renew our pledge of support. . . .

And finally, to those nations who would make themselves our adversary, we offer not a pledge but a request: that both sides begin anew the quest for peace. . . .

Kennedy began six consecutive paragraphs with the same structure; the parallelism heightens the importance and passion of the words and helps make them memorable. The first five repetitions of the pledge help make more memorable the last phrasing, "not a pledge but a request," and sharpen the divide between friend and foe.

- *Synecdoche* is a substitution of the part for the whole, as in a *sail* for the whole ship.
- *Personification* means giving human qualities to inanimate things: *the heavens wept.*
- *Hyperbole* is exaggeration for effect: *Since I ate that cake, I weigh fifty tons. I can't move!*
- *Irony* uses a word to convey its opposite meaning: *I'm so thrilled that you dented my brand-new car!*

· · ·

Each of these devices and figures of speech heightens the emotional content of the words for effect; these are ways of conveying your passion with the words themselves.

8

How to Be Passionate Nonverbally

A sure grasp of nonverbal passion is the essence of charisma and the most important means you have for increasing your charisma quotient.

TRAIN, CARE FOR, AND USE YOUR VOICE

Following is a quick primer in the care and use of the voice; you can spend a lifetime practicing these techniques and improving your vocal tone. The most important thing is to breathe. Leaders who want to communicate authoritatively must learn the authoritative arc and work on resonance and presence. Those are the basics. Passion comes from freeing up the voice to sing like Martin Luther King's.

Showing Passion in Your Voice   There are lots of ways to indicate passion in the voice; chief among them is a rising tone, but a faster pace and a louder volume are also important. And in contrast, you can pause dramatically and get very quiet. The point is to establish a normal voice and then vary it to indicate emotion.

Watch a clip of Martin Luther King Jr.'s "I Have a Dream" speech, which I quoted from in Chapter Seven. King used all three of these vocal means to telegraph his passion. Most remarkable about his voice was the range in pitch: his voice rose in tone so much that it is almost as if sang his words.

Even as King's voice rose, he did not lose his authority. That's an important point to note because so many speakers end their sentences as if they were asking questions. They use a rising tone at the end of every sentence. They introduce themselves, for example, by saying, "Hi, my name is Nick?" as if they weren't sure. The effect is to reduce the information that's coming through the vocal channel. We have a hard enough time as it is to understand each other, and when we can't tell the difference between a question and a statement, it's that much harder.

The Authoritative Arc   Instead of adopting the annoying habit of rising tone at the end of sentences, use the authoritative arc. That's what great public figures do (King did it particularly well), and it's essential if you're going to be an authoritative leader and communicator. In the authoritative arc, your voice starts on one note, hopefully one where your voice is resonant (more about that later), and then rises in pitch through the sentence to indicate your passion. At the end, it drops back down, at least to the note you started from and perhaps even lower. The effect is to remove all doubt from what you're saying.

If you try this, you'll find that people accept your utterances without question—most of the time. If you speak with authority, other people will accept what you say by and large. Try it the next time you want a better room at a hotel, and you'll be surprised at the results. Say, "What do you have that's better than that?" but drop your voice in pitch at the end and watch the clerk jump to offer you an upgrade.

Resonance and Presence   Voices also need resonance and presence. Resonance makes voices pleasant to listen to, and thus persuasive. Presence is that nasal quality of the voice that allows it to be heard. You need both.

For resonance, take a deep bellyful of air, and hold it in with your diaphragmatic muscles, the ones that curve along your rib cage over your navel. Watch opera singers and yoga instructors; they breathe this way. Don't move your shoulders up as you breath in; rather, the motion should be in your belly. It should move out as you take air in, because it's expanding to take in the air.

Most people who don't sing at the Met or bend their bodies in elegant pretzels breathe with their shoulders, and as a result they take in only a quarter or half of a lungful of air. The result is a voice without resonance that's flat, uninspiring, and unpleasant to listen to. Fight that with belly breathing.

It's also calming and grounding to breathe in this way. Before you go into an important meeting with your boss, say, take a breath or two from deep in your belly. You'll be surprised at how much it calms you, and it has the added benefit of giving your voice resonance, which sounds more self-assured and strong. It will get your meeting off to a good start.

For presence, put your hands alongside your nose, open your mouth wide, and make a noise like a sheep bleating: *Baaa. Baaa. Baaa.* You'll find that your nasal passages vibrate, and you'll feel the vibration through your fingers. That's good presence, and it's what allows a voice to carry.

You want a little of that in your voice whenever you're meeting with more than two people so that they can hear you. A quiet voice that people can't hear will be taken as either timidity or incredible confidence, à la the Godfather. Don't take a chance. Get some presence in your voice.

Pitch   Some people pitch their voices too high or too low habitually. That puts a strain on the voice, prevents it from achieving its full authority, and undercuts passion. I worked with one consultant, a frequent speaker, who used a voice when she was speaking that was so high that people called her the "dolphin lady." She was extremely smart, but her career was hampered by her crazy voice, which showed up not in casual conversation but in public speaking and important meetings where she had to hold forth.

All signs pointed to some sort of psychological distress that was causing her to push her voice into the stratosphere, and it was my job to work with her to bring it down to earth. It took a lot of breathing and determination on her part. In the end, we brought in a speech therapist because the pressure of speaking in that high-pitched squeak had damaged her vocal chords.

We began by having her lie down on the floor, relax completely, and begin to speak with proper breathing. It took a lot of work, and in the end it was transformational. You can try this at home by consulting books on the topic; it's very good for the voice.[1]

That's an extreme case, but here's a way you can test your voice to see if it's pitched at your maximum resonance point. Find your way to a keyboard (get help if you're not musically literate). Pick out the lowest note you can comfortably sing, and work your way up to the highest. For most people, that's two octaves: sixteen white notes. (For Mariah Carey, it's five octaves, but that's why she's singing professionally and we're not.)

Now divide the number of white notes you span by four, and count up that number from the bottom. So if it is two octaves, 16 divided by 4 is 4, you start from your bottom note and count up 4. That note is your maximum resonance point. Most of your normal talking should be taking place in and around that note.

Some men push their voices lower to sound more authoritative, and some women push their voices higher so as not to frighten the men. But male or female, you want to be at your resonance point. That will give your voice more authority and timbre, and it will be most pleasant to listen to. It will also extend the life of your voice and avoid damage.

OTHER WAYS TO DEMONSTRATE PASSION

What about the rest of the body? Once again, the closer you get to people, the more energy there is between you, and so the more passion. The motion I discussed in the previous chapter is relevant here too. Also, facial gesture and hand gesture are important. Obviously someone waving her hands around and grimacing looks more passionate than someone standing still and keeping a deadpan face. But passion can be telegraphed through quiet moments too. Just watch a great actor and feel the emotion emanating from him or her in both animated and quiet moments.

Passion is both authentic and charismatic. We don't fully trust people until we've seen them get emotional—angry, sad, ecstatic—because these moments allow us to take the measure of their values. What gets them angry, sad, or ecstatic? That's how we size them up. If we see someone giving a tongue-lashing to a sales clerk because the store is out of an item, we make one kind of judgment about that person. If we see someone else standing up to a bully, we make another kind of judgment.

Sincerity of emotion shows up in nonverbal conversation through, perhaps surprisingly, stillness and openness. While the strong passions—anger, joy, excitement of various kinds—can all be signaled with energetic body movements, sometimes extreme stillness can be just as effective. Think of it like the voice: the point is to establish a baseline and then vary that to exhibit the emotions.

We worked with a speaker who was telling a personal story to a large audience and revealing information that had not been public before. There was a lot of tension on his staff before the big night. We talked with the speaker about many ways that he could indicate his passion to that audience, but in the end we settled on simplicity. He stood very still and told his story very quietly. The passion came through.

That said, for most of us, when we want to telegraph passion, we need to do so with raised voice, higher voice, more hand and arm gestures, more body movement in general—all the signs of energy and passion that we are used to recognizing. But rather than thinking about this as a technical exercise, the better way is to focus on the passion itself. Before you go into an important meeting, begin a high-stakes speech, or have that conversation with your teenager that you've been putting off, focus on the way you feel about the topic and the person or people you're communicating with. This technique has two benefits. First, it will put you in the moment if you do it well, allowing you to connect the two conversations and appear authentic and charismatic. And second, it will occupy your mind and keep you from getting nervous. If you think only about your nerves, your self-consciousness, and how poorly the scene is certain to go, you will almost certainly telegraph nervousness in your second conversation and undercut your own best efforts. So spend a moment outside the room or before the meeting begins feeling the excitement you have over this concept you're about to propose, or the passion you feel for the company and where it's headed, or the love you feel for your teenager who has to understand the importance of a curfew and personal safety.

Being passionate is ultimately about allowing yourself to fully experience the emotion. Inhabit it, revel in it, and soak it up. That way you'll send a consistent message, not a mixed one, and you'll come across as an authentic communicator. If the moment is right, you'll show up charismatically, because someone who is radiating a strong emotion is fascinating, eye-catching, and lit up in a special way that we call charismatic.

Great actors have something they call the offstage beat that they use just before they go onstage. Mediocre actors just walk on and deliver their first lines. But the great ones are already inhabiting the character offstage before they go on. They figure out where the character just came from and what state of mind she was in, and they play that rather than "an actor coming onstage." The result is a fully believable character, and one you can't take your eyes from. You need to develop a little of the same magic, and the way to do it is to prepare, just before the communication, not only what you're going to say but how you feel about it: strongly, fully, and with all your physical being. That, after all, is where passion originates. And that's how you radiate passion, align the two conversations, and convince audiences large and small of your authenticity. If you do it with enough conviction, you will be charismatic.

There remains only the final step, listening to your audience, to consider.

Listening, Part One

How to Listen Verbally—and Charismatically

The final step in the layered process of communicating authentically and charismatically as a leader is at first impression a paradoxical one. Isn't communicating your job, you wonder; shouldn't you be doing something? Listening sounds passive. And anyway, how can that help you get your message across?

A communication consists of a sender (you), a receiver (your audience), a message, a medium, noise (distractions, any problems with communicating), and feedback. At the simplest level, you don't know whether the message has been received unless you get feedback. So listening is a necessary part of the communication game.

At a deeper level, you want to know how clearly and fully the message has gotten through. Does she fully understand the implications of your offer? Has the potential buyer had all his objections answered? Is the speech moving hearts and minds, or are they just applauding politely?

THE NEED FOR FOLLOWERS

A leader's communication is always a two-way activity. Leaders, to be blunt, need followers, and a good leader wants to know what those followers are thinking and doing. Moreover, leaders are always in the business of persuasion, and you need to be listening to the people being persuaded or you won't know how you're doing.

If you think of a persuasive communication as a journey you take your audience (one or one thousand) on to change minds, then you'll see that listening is a vital part of that process too. Changing one's mind occurs in a series of steps, and you need to know what step the other person is on in order to be effective in leading the process.

Finally, there's an even deeper reason that you need to be in the listening business as a leader. I believe that it's the responsibility of a leader to return the courtesy of your followers by making an equivalent effort to listen as hard to them as they do to you. It's courteous and it's right, and it's necessary in the long run if you're going to fulfill the leader's full set of obligations.

I've worked with leaders who respect their followers and leaders who despise their followers. The latter, frankly, don't do as well and don't last as long as the others. At some level, they must despise themselves, or why would they bother to lead people they can't respect?

Good listening, then, is a profound activity. People need to be heard to be validated as human. We're a social species.

Listening has both a verbal and a nonverbal component. I examine the verbal in this chapter and deal with the nonverbal in the next.

FEEDBACK

At its most basic, good listening offers feedback.[1] Feedback, which is often critical, is simply a response, usually involving evaluation of some kind.

Many leaders, in fact, consider (critical) feedback the beginning and end of their job in terms of communicating to their followers. I worked with one CEO who believed that it was enough to tell his executive team when they had screwed up. "They have a job to do; they're paid a salary. Why should I praise them?" I finally persuaded him to broaden his communications palate for the purely transactional reason that it would get him better results. He was dragged kicking and screaming into a more enlightened version of communication, but he wasn't thrilled about it. It seemed like work to him. His career did not prosper, though in the short term, he got high marks for listening. Too bad he didn't believe it worked and relapsed into the transactional model.

So feedback both good and critical is an essential part of listening. Here's how to do it without destroying the ego of the receiver and ultimately the relationship. Begin by describing the actions of the person to whom you're giving feedback: "You completed the task on Tuesday." If your purpose is critical, relate the action to the standard: "It was due on Monday." Then describe the consequences of the behavior, and the reasons for them: "Being a day late leads to bottlenecks at the plant and will cost us forty-five thousand dollars each time.

We can't afford that kind of cost and stay in business." Then make your request: "I need you to complete the task on time in the future." Finally, check for comprehension and agreement: "Do you understand? Can you commit to getting the task completed by Monday from now on?"

The key is to avoid all the tempting analyses and speculations on the motivation of the receiver. This is known colloquially as *glomming* and involves generalizing, justly or not, from the specific example: "You always turn your project in late! Are you deliberately trying to sabotage us? Do you want to screw us? Are you trying to bring the organization down? Are you drinking again?" These sorts of communications, satisfying as they may be, crowd the channel with emotional baggage that ultimately gets in the way of persuasion. It's difficult, but don't tell the person that he or she is bad. Instead, stick to the facts and the consequences.

So it's possible to give feedback well, both the good and bad variety. But if you want your audience to feel that it has been heard, feedback isn't really enough. Too often, it feels punitive, despite your best efforts, and it certainly feels like it's judgmental.

PARAPHRASING

To go a little further as a good listener, try paraphrasing what your audience is saying. This activity is surprisingly difficult for the poor listeners of the world. For the rest of us, it's easy enough if we can swallow the temptation to give our own opinions.

Paraphrasing means simply saying something like, "So let me be sure I've understood. What you're saying is that the green ones are tastier than the brown ones?" The point is to play back, like a recorder, what the person has said to you. That's all. Resist the temptation to embroider (*"But that's ridiculous! That can't be true!"*) because that undoes all the good work of the paraphrase.

Paraphrasing is a powerful technique because it gets your receiver agreeing with you. He or she nods and says, "Yes, that's correct. That's what I said." From that simple agreement, you can build a persuasive relationship because you've begun to create trust and liking. It's impossible to hate or distrust completely someone whom you've just agreed with, especially in the act of replaying your wise words back to you.

This is important, and it's simple. And yet many people seem to be incapable of doing it. It all begins with letting the other person know that he or she has been heard. It's not taxing intellectually, provided you have been listening. Many people spend the time when the other person is talking thinking about what they're going to say next. Thus, they don't really hear what's been said. For them, paraphrasing is very difficult, but it is a useful discipline.

CLARIFYING

Now let's take the game higher. A subtle improvement on paraphrasing is clarifying what the speaker has said while essentially repeating it back to him. For example, your boss says to you, "Look, Gillian, things aren't working out with you in your new role here. What's going on is that we have to separate the fish from the head, you know what I mean? It's just not going to work this way. We have to, you know, separate the fish from the head. Let's have a trial period. Ninety days.

We can't go on like this. It's not working." What you say is something like this: "So what I hear you saying, Jim, is that you're putting me on a ninety-day-trial period."[2] This is a real example from a client, and of course an extreme one.

Most of the time, you don't have to provide such heroic feats of listening and translation. The point is to translate and clarify what the other person is saying and play it back in order to check understanding. This is much harder work than merely paraphrasing, because you have to think hard about what you've heard and offer a fair summary or restatement. Why do it? What's the advantage to the communication process?

There are several possibilities. Often the other person will be verbose or vague, or both, in her wording, and summary restatements offer the chance to provide welcome clarity to the discussion.

Clarification is also a subtle way to take control of the discussion. For example, if you're having a meeting with several people, you can guide and moderate the discussion by summarizing and clarifying to get agreement among the various parties: "So, Joan wants to go forward, but with significant modifications to the plan. Bill wants the plan, pure and simple, without modification. And Frances wants to throw the plan out and start again. Is that a fair summary of where everyone stands?" If you can get agreement to that statement, you haven't solved the overall disagreement, but you've provided the basis for going forward.

A more subtle possibility is to gently reshape what people are saying in order to move them slowly toward a point of view or an outcome you desire: "So if I can find some common ground here, it seems that we have, broadly speaking, three camps. Alice and the folks over here are thinking about new possibilities: growing our way back to profitability. Jack and these people are mainly focused on cost-cutting. And the ladies and gentlemen sitting back there with Alfredo want to take the company private. Is that a fair statement of where everyone stands?"

In reaction to a statement like this, typically you'll get some further clarification ("We also want to cut costs; we're just saying there's no way you're going to get to $7 billion without something new") but agreement in the main. If you've made a fair and honest attempt to summarize the various positions you're concerned with, you will rarely get rebellion.

The point is that this kind of statement allows you to lead the discussion forward in the context and with the items on the table that you want to address. It's a matter of letting others be heard but insisting that you remain in control. And yet if you do it well, most people react positively and do not feel as if they have been railroaded or even guided. But you must be genuine and not distort people's positions. You get to set the context, the frame. You remain in charge.

This kind of active listening is hard work. You have to be completely clear about your position and secure in your role. And you have to be closely attuned to everyone else's body language—their implicit nonverbal communications—as well as what they're saying out loud. You don't want people to feel unfairly represented and not tell you, because that will make the possibility of reaching ultimate agreement more difficult. Most reasonable people will agree in the end to compromise without feeling victimized if and only if they believe they've been heard.

EMPATHIC LISTENING

So far, we've been dealing with the surface level of communication: the ostensible meaning of the words that are said. To really begin to listen, you need to hear, see, and reflect the deeper, emotional meanings of the dialogue. This level might be called empathic listening. Here, you identify the emotion underneath the words and respond in kind: "I understand how painful this is for you, Joseph. I too had a project go bad early in my career. It really hurts." Note that this response first identifies, and accurately, the pain that the other person is feeling and then takes it on, sharing a similar experience or emotion from your own life story to identify with the other. That's empathy.

The danger with empathy is that it loses its powerful connecting effect if the empathic listener goes on too long with his own story. If your tale of your bad project rambles on for several minutes, the other folks will feel that their moment has been hijacked for your own purposes, and the good work of your empathy will go down the tubes.

Nonetheless, empathic listening can be extraordinarily powerful because if you can bond with your listeners over shared emotional experiences, they will allow you to suggest a path forward. It's why Alcoholics Anonymous is a successful organization. If I have a problem, I'm not likely to accept your words of wisdom on the subject if I don't feel you know at least as well as I do what we're talking about.

This can lead to absurd forms of one-upmanship, so you need to keep your urge under control to be the most important victim, or star, in the room. The point is to tactfully say that you understand the other person's feeling without in the least diminishing it or overtopping it. Remember that the most powerful kind of listening is deeply empathic and analytical.

Finally, the most powerful form of listening—the one that people most strongly react to, feeling that they are both heard and understood—is a form of empathic listening where you identify the emotion and state its underlying causes without trying to solve the problem. "So, Bill, what I hear you saying is that you're angry with me because I haven't fully appreciated the lengths you've gone to in trying to win over our Latin American customers. Those efforts have caused you a lot of sleepless nights, time away from the family, and marital problems. Is that right?"

Don't try to solve the problem at this stage. Just acknowledge it fully, and you will be surprised at how powerful that acknowledgment is for the other person. The key elements are the correct identification of the emotion; the reasons for it, including your own personal responsibility, if any; and a full statement of the facts of the situation if those haven't been brought up openly before.

This form of active listening—active because you're acknowledging your own role in the situation—is the hardest to undertake. In a contentious situation, it can feel as if you're giving in to openly express how the other is feeling. But you're not; you're just stating the other's position as fully and honestly as you can. Agreement, compromise, or resolution will come later. For now, active listening is a powerful first step toward solving any serious problem in a communication.

What you will find is that if you've done it well, people will agree profoundly and powerfully with you. Of course, to accomplish this form of listening effectively, you must be good at reading the emotions of others, and those come chiefly from the nonverbal conversation. What you're doing is translating the nonverbal into the verbal, and that is an important and difficult skill for any leader who wishes to have a full set of tools for persuasive communications.

Listening, Part Two

How to Listen
Nonverbally—and
Charismatically

How do you listen nonverbally? What does that even mean? Beyond the obvious idea that you listen with your ears, what else is there?

LISTEN WITH YOUR WHOLE BODY

I always challenge clients to listen with their whole body. That means quieting your own activity as a first step, so that you won't be distracted and you'll show the other person that you're not distracted. Both are equally essential.

The deep reason for listening with your whole body is that you're aligning your two conversations in the listening mode just as you do when you're talking. If you ask for feedback or ask someone a question but your nonverbal conversation is busy doing something else, you're telling the other person very powerfully that you don't really care what he is saying.

Thus, your nonverbal orientation should not only be still, but it should be directed toward the other person or persons. You can't listen adequately unless your torso is oriented toward the other person and your body language is open and connected. There is no faster way to shut someone off than by giving a cold shoulder.

Because the nonverbal conversation is so important to our ability to communicate with one another, if you don't listen with your whole body, you won't hear everything that's being said.

People know unconsciously the moment you begin to move on in terms of listening. They may not realize it consciously at first, but unconsciously it's immediate. You'll see responses like moving nearer, grabbing an arm, raising the voice—all the activities that people use when they want to connect or reconnect.

THIN-SLICING

One of the most pernicious concepts widely circulated about listening is in the otherwise admirable book *Blink*. Malcolm Gladwell introduces the idea of what he calls thin-slicing as a way of talking about how a very small sample can stand for a whole host of evidence under specific circumstances and conditions. Unfortunately, he equates the thin-slicing idea with the expert's ability to instantly size up, for example, an ancient statue as real or fake because of a myriad clues unconsciously weighed, evaluated, and sorted. Here is what Gladwell wrote:

In September of 1983, an art dealer by the name of Gianfranco Becchina approached the J. Paul Getty

Museum in California. He had in his possession, he said, a marble statue dating from the sixth century B.C. It was what is known as a kouros—a sculpture of a nude male youth standing with his left leg forward and his arms at his side. There are only about two hundred kouroi in existence, and most have been recovered badly damaged. . . . But this one was almost perfectly preserved. . . . It was an extraordinary find. Becchina's asking price was just under $10 million.

The Getty moved cautiously. It . . . began a thorough investigation. . . .

A geologist from the University of California . . . spent two days examining the surface of the statue with a high-resolution stereomicroscope. . . . [He] concluded . . . the statue was old. It wasn't some contemporary fake. . . .

The kouros, however, had a problem. It didn't look right. The first to point this out was an Italian art historian named Federico Zeri. . . . He found himself staring at the sculpture's fingernails. In a way he couldn't immediately articulate, they seemed wrong to him.[1]

Other experts weighed in, and the statue was finally judged a fake. The Getty was embarrassed, and the art world had a great story to tell.

What does this have to do with listening? The idea has lodged in the public mind that somehow we can all be expert thin-slicers based on a quick look, a brief listen, a glancing moment of attention. But Gladwell has confused our ability to make snap (because unconscious) nonverbal judgments about the intent of people and the danger quotient of situations we're thrown in, with an expert's ability, when her learning is profound, to size up something quickly. The result has been that too many people now say, "Just let me thin-slice this."

The only thing we're doing there is getting a quick read on our impression of the other person's intent. We are pretty good at it, but we can certainly be wrong, and it is most emphatically not the same as expertise in a field like art history. They're two completely different activities. The former is almost entirely unconscious and instant, whereas the latter is primarily conscious but drawing on an unconscious sifting of the physical evidence brought to the conscious mind. And it often is a slow process, where something niggles at the back of the mind for days before the expert is able to become fully aware of what is going on. That is what in fact happens to several of the experts in Gladwell's fake masterpiece story. They take weeks to figure out why the statue doesn't seem real to them or to piece together their analysis, impressions, and unconscious deciphering.

My point is this: we can't listen to other people by thin-slicing them. Listening takes time. When it is done right, it is primarily an emotional activity and only secondarily intellectual. Emotions take time to express, be heard, be validated, and so on.

To listen well and deeply to another person, you must quiet your own two conversations, and let your verbal and your non-verbal channels attend to what's being said to you. Listen with your whole body. It's fast becoming an old-fashioned courtesy, but no less essential for leaders because of that. Followers who are not listened to will not follow forever.

A WANNABE CFO WHO LACKED ESSENTIAL SKILLS

I worked with a client (call him Bill) who was hoping to win a big promotion to chief financial officer (CFO). He was a smart, successful financial manager who had been with the company for a number of years, and he had the support of the charismatic CEO who had founded and still ran the company.

But he had failed to win the confidence of the board during the opportunities he had been given by the current CFO to present financial information to it. The board recognized his intelligence but didn't feel that he was executive material. Moreover, the company had a family feel and valued its social activities highly. Everyone from the board on down was expected to take part in parties, outings, picnics, and other activities. But Bill didn't enjoy the social whirl that the company involved its employees in, and he was not very good at taking part. He tended to stand to one side of the group during a cocktail party, say, and look at his watch frequently. Not very engaging behavior.

The CEO asked me to improve Bill's ability to interact with others. This was a tall challenge, given that Bill had developed his solitary style over forty years of living. His habits, psychological needs, and avoidance of crowds were well established. I knew it was not going to be easy, even if Bill wanted to change.

And Bill did. He accepted that he had to become more of a social butterfly if he was to win the CFO's chair and the confidence of the board. He resented the fuss a little, but he was determined to improve.

We worked for some time on Bill's expressiveness. The 360-degree evaluation data made it clear that his coworkers both above and below him on the organization chart felt that he was cold, not very expressive, reserved, and hard to read. His fellow employees had various ways of expressing their concerns, but it all added up to a feeling that he was not a very giving man.

In role-plays of Bill's interactions with his employees and talking about the origins of his inexpressiveness, it became clear that he was not so much shy as guarded. It was dangerous, in his mind, to reveal what he was feeling. As a result, his underlings saw him as censorious and his supervisors as defensive. His need for safety, ironically, was going to cost him his career.

The same issues were surfacing at home too. His wife began telling him that he was emotionally cold and distant, and she threatened divorce.

Bill felt a little put upon by all this fuss. He was just playing it safe. Why did he have to show his hand? He didn't expect others to emote all over him and didn't enjoy it when they did, so why should he have to?

It was almost as if Bill was lacking something basic in the way of connectedness with his fellow human beings. But what was to be done? He had the need, and to an extent the desire, to improve his ability to relate to his coworkers and his family. At least, he fully appreciated the cost of not improving. But how to make significant strides in a short time? And what was the best thing to focus on?

As Bill watched the tape of himself in our role-playing situations, he was able to recognize that he was doing less than the rest of us to hold up his end of the social contract. But the effort it cost him to work harder was enormous. He had to learn skills quickly that most people master over the first third of their lives. He complained that there was too much to think about: nodding, smiling, raising his eyebrows, and so on. And that was just his face. Then there were his gestures, his body language, and all the rest. It was just too much to do, he felt, to become a charismatic executive overnight.

We had been preparing for a couple of months for a big presentation to the board, one for which he had been informed the stakes were high. If he didn't show great improvement at this event, his career at the company was over. And his wife was giving him months, and not much more, to start being a better husband.

A cocktail party for the executive team, the board, and some local dignitaries was scheduled for the night before the board presentation. Bill had been told that the presentation was the moment of truth, but he suspected that if he didn't show up at the party as a new man, personable, lively, and even charismatic, nothing he could do at the board meeting would help much. Those cocktail parties were the real testing ground for the C-suite.

Bill was now beginning to panic. He was making progress on his facial gestures and appearing more forthcoming generally, but the progress was modest, and he tended to relapse in moments of stress. His fear, and mine, was that he would freeze at the party or the meeting, and it would all be over.

It was time for more drastic measures. So I decided to make a listener out of Bill because listening is at the heart of real charisma. He had to show some more animation so that the board (and his wife) didn't write him off as a loser, but that was taking too long. What he could learn to do quickly was to make a virtue of his guardedness and start watching others even more closely.

We added a device to the mix: I told Bill to get a digital camera and start taking pictures at the cocktail party. He would start a new section on the company Web site documenting their sociability, of which they were inordinately proud. And then we practiced several kinds of listening. He needed no work on the first kind of listening: feedback. He was already critical enough. So I made Bill paraphrase everything I said and then clarify over and over again as he got the hang of paraphrasing. Soon he was delving into my emotional state in greater and greater depth and sophistication as he listened actively for my emotions and the reasons underlying them.

The combination of listening and the camera changed Bill's ability to interact with others. Although he was only slowly improving in terms of his own expressiveness, the quality of his interactions with others improved markedly because there is nothing so flattering as the feeling that you are being listened to.

Bill is now a well-respected CFO—at another company. At the new company, he has a reputation for being selfless. That's because he has become such a great listener. The whole process took longer than the first company would give him, but he did get there in the end.

PUT A POWERFUL TOOL TO WORK

How do you put this powerful tool to work for you in improving your leadership communication? As I've said, leaders must be great listeners. The ability validates for your followers the faith that they put in you. Just as you focused on your own emotions while discovering and mastering the passion that is essential for authentic leadership, now you must learn to focus on the emotions of the people you are communicating with. This is the last, and in some ways the most important, step to achieving authenticity as a communicator, and it is, counter-intuitively, also essential for achieving charisma.

You must learn to read others' emotions. When you listen with your whole body, using your intuition or unconscious to read the emotions of those with whom you're communicating, the result is a connection with the other people in the room that they experience as engaging, fascinating, and indeed charismatic.

Why is this the case? Why should focusing on someone else's emotional state add to your charisma? Technically, the outward focus that you must adopt will contribute to your stillness, which, when it is combined with energy, is charismatic. More than that, as you establish and maintain a connection with the others in the room, they will experience this as a heightened interest in you.

This is the kind of magic that candidate Bill Clinton exhibited on the campaign trail during his two runs for the White House. He would establish strong eye contact with a questioner and, holding his whole body still as he focused on the person, raise his eyebrows, open his eyes, and nod. All the while, he'd be moving as close as he could to the questioner. The effect was powerful, partly because of Clinton's technical mastery of all the details of gesture but mostly because of the quality of his listening. The strength of the bond that he would establish with one questioner would, by proxy, be felt by all of the people in the room. That's charisma.

Think of it this way. Your job as a persuasive leader communicating with an individual or group of people is most often to move them to some kind of action. To do that, you have to change their minds. You're taking them, in effect, from point A to point B. That movement is not only intellectual but also, and more fundamentally, emotional. So your job as a listener is to figure out what your audience's emotional state is at the beginning of your communication and then monitor the progress of that emotional state as you move them on the journey to action.

To put it as simply as possible, where are they emotionally when you first meet with them, and where are they when you're done? If you've been persuasive, you've moved them from passive acceptance of the current condition, or anger at it, or frustration with it to a refocused energy about changing it. The act of listening to your audience, whether of one or one thousand or more, is monitoring that progress from passive to active, from why to how, from emotion turned inward to emotion turned outward.

What you'll find when you do the work of listening hard to the people you communicate with is that you will quickly become more attuned to others' emotional states and they will soon become more enthralled with you. They will welcome you showing up because you will be the leader who pays the most attention to them, and that commodity is as scarce as platinum in this information-saturated age.

Don't ever thin-slice the job of listening to your followers and the people around you. That's where the real currency of charisma is to be acquired. Invest in listening, and it will repay you manyfold.

How to Read
Others

W e are all unconscious experts in reading other people's intentions toward us. We learned these skills, the idea goes, in the woolly mammoth era because our lives depended on them. But we are not very good at making this unconscious awareness *conscious* in ways useful to our information age. We can react with blinding speed, literally before we can think, to duck a punch that some drunken lout throws in our direction, or to hop out of the way of an oncoming object. That's a good thing; it's unconscious, and it works. But we are far less adept in general at noting consciously what everyone else in a meeting is really thinking, say, or evaluating who the chief ringleaders are in the party that's against your plan for expansion, for example.

Yet those intentions are there to see. The problem is that, far from too little information about how others are feeling, you actually get too much. People are constantly shifting, twitching, looking up, down, and sideways, raising their eyebrows, narrowing their eyes, scratching their noses. What does it all mean? How can you possibly monitor all of it in a room of ten people, or many more, and do so in time to react appropriately?

You can't. It is too much information, too fast, and there is too much chaff intermixed with the wheat. Is Jane stroking her chin because she's pondering your proposal? Or is she merely scratching an itchy chin as surreptitiously as she can? Is Jack folding his arms because he's resisting your best attempts to talk the whole group into changing direction, or is he merely cold? You can make yourself crazy trying to consciously monitor the constantly changing body signals of a roomful of people to little avail, because by the time you sort it all out, the conversation has moved on. Meanwhile, you haven't been attending to the content of the conversation as closely as you probably need to.

Is there a way around this dilemma of needing to monitor gigabytes of streaming data about people's intentions consciously and rapidly, while at the same paying close attention to the content of the conversations? There is. If, rather than monitoring the data generally, you look for confirmation of your own hypotheses about intention, then you can speed up and narrow the stream of information you need to take in.

So the real question is this: If you want to become a conscious expert in reading other people's unconscious expression of their intent, how do you form hypotheses about that expression and confirm or reject them? The answer is to restrict your possible hypotheses to a few that you've identified before your meeting, conversation, or presentation. Then you can pose the single question to your subconscious mind and use that unconscious expertise we all have to give you a clear, reliable answer.

There are five possible continua along which to locate others' intents:

open—closed

sincere—insincere

allied—opposed

powerful—subservient

committed—uncommitted[1]

You can, of course, add your own for specific situations that these don't cover, but you'll find that these work with most human interactions where you need to monitor body language in detail.

I'll examine each continuum in turn. The idea is to spend some time thinking about the nonverbal conversation in an upcoming interaction—an important one—and choose the continuum that most closely fits what you're worried about or interested in, or represents the crux of the issue between you and the others involved.

For example, when the nation watched President Bill Clinton insist, "I did not have sex with that woman," we really cared only to know whether he was lying.[2] Was he sincere or insincere? We needed to monitor the host of signals around truth and lies. Anyone doing so would have picked up some reasonably reliable indicators that the president was lying. Chief among them was a sudden burst of anger and an uncharacteristic jab of the forefinger in the often-replayed video clip. Both of these were good indicators that the president was concealing something. Hence, he was lying. But more about this continuum in its place.

THE OPEN—CLOSED CONTINUUM

The first of the continua, or possible hypotheses, about others' intentions is the most basic one. Indeed, with a little practice, you should be able to size people up very quickly along these lines on an almost automatic basis. Don't think of this as thin-slicing, however, because it takes some time to establish a baseline of behavior with each new person you meet. The point is not to be able to perform this task instantly, but to be able to size someone up within a few minutes, with high reliability, in terms of whether this person is open to you.

This is a good one to begin with because an earlier chapter explored the nonverbal communication of openness. You should already be well on the way toward being an expert in others' openness (or not) as well as your own.

In this section, we look more deeply at the verbal and nonverbal expression of openness in order to give you the fullest possible range of human behavior to compare to when you're putting this technique into practice.

Let's begin with the face. First, notice the forehead. Is it wrinkled or smooth? For most of us, our habitual state of open versus closed attitudes is expressed in our foreheads, especially after about age thirty. The more wrinkles and the deeper they are, the more habitually open a person is likely to be. This is because a characteristic gesture of the open person is to raise the eyebrows, wrinkling the forehead, when looking for a response. Over the years, if you spend a good deal of time openly inviting response, you'll get forehead wrinkles.

There are fakers, but on the whole the forehead is a reliable sign of overall orientation. That does not mean that a person will be open or closed in any particular instance, but it does give you a sense of his or her general receptivity.

Beyond the forehead, notice the mobility of the eyebrows. How often and far do they move? People tend to raise their eyebrows when they're interacting with others: looking for a response, asking a question, taking you in, and so on. So the amount and distance of motion are indicators of a general level of openness, and in the specific instance, when the eyebrows are up, openness to your input in the moment. Again, the movement may be in response to a question that the person has asked you, but it's openness nonetheless.

Now go down to the eyes themselves. Are they narrowed or wide open? You need to establish a baseline of how the person behaves in fairly neutral situations. That will give you an idea of whether the particular case is one of openness. Generally people open their eyes wider when they are interested in something or someone and close them when they are not, or are actively suspicious or wary of events, people, or actions.

Because people are so active with their eyes, you need to be careful to rule out environmental reasons. Is a bright light shining in the person's face? That may account for narrowed eyes. It may not be because you've just offered the person a used car at an unbeatable price. If you can, look at the pupils. How open or shut are they? Openness indicates interest, attraction, and arousal; the opposite indicates the reverse. Of course, the general level of lighting in the environment also affects the pupils, so you need to establish a benchmark, a norm.

Move on to the nose. Flaring nostrils are the stuff of romance novels and books about horses. Nevertheless, there may be truth to the descriptions connecting sexual attraction to this part of the face, especially if research about pheromones and attraction turns out to be true.[3]

It is certainly the case that a wrinkled nose can indicate disgust, or at the very least disgust at a bad smell. Extreme facial gestures like these are hard to miss and easily brought to the conscious. It is the subtler ones you should be more concerned with. By the time someone gets to the point of wrinkling his nose, he's probably already told you how he feels or is just about to do so.

The mouth is capable of a thousand variations on the basic retinue of smile, frown, surprise, fear, and so on. In simple terms, look for the smile. That's the universally understood sign of approval from others, and thus people who are smiling are more likely to be open to you than people who are neutral or frowning. But of course people can smile for other reasons; once again context is important to be able to distinguish a rigid, unhappy, or false smile from a relaxed, natural one that is welcoming and open.

Think about the whole face for a moment. How we orient our heads toward each other in space is extraordinarily revealing of our degree of openness toward one another. I recently saw a news clip of two politicians meeting. The one was a presidential candidate, the other a potential endorsement the candidate was eagerly courting. The clip was brief, but as the two sat in side-by-side chairs, the potential endorser's head was tipped back and away from the candidate. My take was that there would be no good news that night. As it turned out, the news came the next day, and the endorsement was not forthcoming; the vote went to the other candidate. In that case, the head told the story.

We move our heads away and out of the plane of the other person, either up or down, when we're thinking or withdrawing in some way—from anger, fear, or a host of other possible negative emotions. In this case, once the person is done thinking, watch where the head goes. If the person makes strong eye contact and turns her head back toward yours, the answer is yes. Otherwise the answer may be no.

If the other person is a spouse or close friend, the *underlying* message may be something like, "I still love you, but the answer's no this one time." In that case, the head may signal yes to the loved one in order to stress that the other person doesn't want to change the underlying relationship, just signal an answer in the current discussion.

For the torso, nearness and direction signal degrees of openness. Fundamentally, the closer and more directly oriented the other's torso is toward you, the more open that person is, and the farther away and more turned away from you, the more closed.

Hand gestures speak a similar language. When people reach toward us with open gestures, they're usually signaling openness. Only rarely is it something else, like a left hook to the jaw. An embrace, the ultimate open gesture, is a combination of open hand gestures and open torso.

All of these gestures are obvious in intent. But when you combine socially prescribed gestures with unconscious behavior, things get interesting. When two people shake hands, for example, it's not terribly revealing because it's a practice we all learn in Western culture. But watch the other hand. What is it doing? If the message from the other hand is not open, you may want to be on your guard. Did the other hand clench, go behind the back, or in the pocket? Be careful in that case. This person has something else on his or her mind.

When we're wrapped in a double handshake, it feels particularly all-embracing precisely because both hands are involved, and we don't have to worry what the other hand is doing. That's why politicians use it, and other people who really want to signal their openness to you.

Openness can be read in the hand itself as well. What is it doing? Is it clenched or nervously kneading the other hand? Is it twitchy or attempting to conceal itself in a pocket? Hands speak an endless and fascinating language; they are marvelous little weathervanes to the state of the soul within and its intents. If you make a practice of watching other people's hands, you'll learn about the state of their nerves, their defensiveness, their confidence, their anger, their happiness, their sorrow, their interest or boredom, in addition to their openness or lack thereof.

Many books on body language purport to give specific meanings of specific gestures, but this is a fool's game. Each gesture can have a multitude of meanings. We cross our arms, to pick a simple example, because we're defensive, to be sure, but also because we're tired, we're cold, or we want to hide an expanding belly.

If you're looking for the answer to a specific question, then you can put that unconscious expertise to work for you. Ask yourself, *Is this person open or closed toward me?* Then start looking for the clues that you need to make a determination.

The best way to do this is to pose the question to your subconscious mind first. Ask yourself at the beginning of the conversation, *Open or closed?* and wait for your intuition about the matter to become clear. Once you have a sense of the situation, you can start looking consciously for clues to confirm or negate your initial reading.

Suppose you're at a job interview, and you want to know what your chances of success are. The first question you might want to consider is whether you are even in the running. In other words, is this a real interview or a courtesy interview? So begin the interview asking yourself, *Is this person open or closed to me?* If the answer comes back *closed*, then you can be reasonably sure that someone else already has the job. If the person seems open, you can turn on your energy and charm. You may want to be on the lookout for a change in that reading. What if the interviewer has been open for, say, the first forty-five minutes of the interview and then suddenly starts to send out closed signals? It might be time to change tactics or cut the interview short.

Has the interviewer made up her mind in the negative, or is she simply signaling that the time is up? You may want to ask some specific process questions (out loud) to see, such as, "What's the next step? How will you go about making a decision?" Then the question to ask your unconscious mind is, *Open or closed?* If the answer is given in a closed way, you probably won't get the job. If the body language at that point is open, you are still in the running. A bolder question in that same situation might be to ask, "How do I stack up against the other applicants?" Be prepared for both an answer you like and one you may not like!

Because adults become more or less adept in controlling their faces and upper bodies, it's worth looking at the legs and feet for each of the continua. Often someone has composed his or her face in a friendly greeting, but the legs and feet (and the torso too) may tell a different story. The legs may be crossed away from you, signaling a closed orientation, or the torso may be twisted away, or the other person may simply increase the distance, even slightly, between the two of you.

Once again, include this information in your overall picture. The idea is to get as clear a reading as possible from your subconscious mind and then check it against some conscious data if necessary. Your unconscious reading is likely to be more reliable than your conscious one until you've practiced the latter quite a bit and have become expert in watching the other's behavior. Lean on your unconscious mind first. It can pick up the subtle signals that would take far too long to describe here. It can read tiny changes in body orientation during a conversation, for example, as the other person warms up and cools down to you and your persuasive efforts.

For simplicity, I've given all of these examples in terms of individual conversations. But when there are several people in the room or several score, the process is not essentially different. You just need to ask your subconscious mind to work harder, so scan more widely. Ask yourself, *How am I doing? Is the meeting open or closed to me?* Then look around the room for data for your subconscious. Note what each person is doing and ask yourself, *What does it mean?* It takes a little longer to get a sense of a roomful of people, but your unconscious will provide it if you give it a chance.

You may want to focus more on one or two people if you know they are important decision makers or people the others automatically defer to. If you're in a room of toadies and one or two kingpins, then all the toadies will be exquisitely tuned to pleasing the kingpins. The unconscious expertise of the low-status people will be focused on the powerful as if life depended on it. You can focus on them too, and use the toadies for confirmation of your reading.

THE SINCERE–INSINCERE CONTINUUM

More ink has been spilled on the subject of determining whether other people are lying than any other aspect of body language. But there's only one authority worth reading.[4] Paul Ekman has taken the study of liars and lying out of the dark ages into the light of modern science and reason. Read his work for a fuller exposition on the subject, and how little we actually know, but I'll cover the basics here, adding my own insights where appropriate.

My only fundamental disagreement with Ekman is the most basic one: Ekman says that we can't tell liars—that is, insincerity—with any precision. His work with the CIA and the FBI has improved their performance in detecting when criminals and terrorists are concealing things, but only to a limited extent. And what he says is that you can't tell the lie, but you can tell when someone is concealing a strong emotion. That's what he focuses his research on.

This focus works well for criminals and terrorists in several ways. First, you can improve your ability, with training, to pick out the people in the security line at the airport who are concealing strong emotions. Of course, that will include type A people who are running very late, your Aunt Minnie who is terrified of flying, and terrorists. You can then pull all these folks aside for more questioning.

It's a pretty good approach. But for those of us whose lives run more to the mundane questions of meetings, spouses, and teenagers, we really do want to be able to tell when people are lying to us. Sincere or insincere is an important determination to make. Is the boss telling me straight that she doesn't have any information on upcoming layoffs, or not? I need to know, because I don't want to reassure my team and have them feel let down later, never to trust me again. Is my spouse telling the truth when she says she was working late, or not? Is the teenager who's living in our house drug ridden or merely sleep deprived?

Ekman says that we can't make determinations with any reliability about lying, but I disagree. He's working with the FBI and strangers. He's very concerned about pathological liars, who are very good at concealing the traditional signs of lying, because they're a real problem for the CIA, the police, and the FBI. But we care about people we know well, for the most part, or at least are going to spend some time with. We have, or can get, a good amount of information on their normal behavior, and so we can determine with pretty good reliability when they are lying. And the good news is that the traditionally described clues for lying are reasonably accurate. Once again, it's something you need to turn over to your unconscious mind.

Start with the eyes. If you see the clichéd and obvious clues to lying—twitchy eyes, lack of eye contact—you've got a pretty good sign of deception. For most of us, who deal with normal, decent people most of the time, lying is an uncomfortable activity. We don't like to do it, and so we signal our discomfort with twitchy eyes and so on.

But also look for the opposite taken to an unusual extreme. If you know the person well, look for an attempt to control the eyes (and the rest of behavior) with unnatural stillness. If you're getting wide-eyed innocence suddenly from a teen who hasn't looked you full in the face for weeks, then she's probably lying about where she went with the car last night.

Ekman's main work, and where he's most useful for those of us who have to deal with ordinary people and situations, is with what he calls "micro expressions." These are sudden, very brief betrayals of the main expression of the person with counterexpressions. So if a person is looking at you with a composed, serene face and then a fleeting sneer suddenly crosses his lips, suspect some underlying emotion of disgust or disagreement, for example, that belies the happy face.

These micro expressions last for only an instant, and at first you'll find them hard to spot. But with practice, you can pick up on them. Ekman sells a DVD to help you to hone your skills. With a couple of weeks of training a few hours a day, you can become expert in reading micro expressions.[5]

Another way to approach this is with the unconscious mind. Look at the whole face, and ask yourself, *Sincere or insincere?* Then let your subconscious go to work. It's very good at picking up whether the whole face adds up to a consistent expression. For example, is the mouth set in a smile but the eyes are cold? Insincere. Are the eyes fixed on you with beguiling stillness but the hands are nervously intertwining? Insincere.

Beyond the face itself is the orientation of the head. Most of us, when we lie, turn our head away or tip it up or down so as to move it away from the other person. This is why you don't want to focus too much on specific gestures, but rather let your unconscious mind pick up on the general situation. If you look too much at the eyes, for example, you may miss the fact that the head is turned down and to one side. So ask yourself, *Is this person sincere or insincere?* And then take in the whole person. You'll be able to tell most of the time.

Generally you'll be able to pick up on the attitude of the other person right away, especially if it's a loved one. I had a cancer scare a while back, a condition that turned out fortunately to be benign, but the morning that I came back from the doctor, my wife instantly asked me when I walked in the door, "What's the matter?" She knew something was wrong because my whole body radiated concern.

With lying, look for that overall sense of feeling, the most reliable way to tell. Beyond the eyes and face, look for the torso to be turned away (lying) or toward you (truth). See if there are defensive gestures from the hands and arms and signs of agitation from the hands and fingers. And look for contradictory behavior from the legs and feet. If your spouse says, "No, everything's fine," but his feet are oriented strangely or his legs are awkwardly crossed away from you, those are signs to check into his story further.

With lying, too, listen for signs of strain in the voice. If the voice is carefully controlled or a little higher pitched than usual, the person may be attempting to conceal something. Ekman has found that people who are lying slow down (in an effort to control) their voice and even their facial gestures and other mannerisms. But ordinary people can also rush to get through an awkward-feeling moment. So the main thing to look for is variation from the norm, which you should know well.

THE ALLIED–OPPOSED CONTINUUM

The basic body language to look for to determine whether people are allied to you or opposed, is overall orientation.[6] This makes for entertaining people watching. Once you're on to this aspect of behavior, you'll find it's easy to pick up.

Quite simply, people who are in agreement tend to mirror one another's behavior. One will lead, and the other will follow. This is especially easy to tell when there are three people present, and you want to figure out who's on your side and who isn't. Look for the one who has the same basic body orientation as you. For a test, move and see if the other person follows suit in the next thirty seconds.

Spouses, partners, and lovers usually mirror one another's physical orientation when they're together or with others and they're in basic agreement. It's interesting to watch couples for signs of mirroring—and its opposite. You can often detect trouble in the relationship before the couple is aware of it.

What happens in mirroring is more profound than just agreement or even connection, however. Because persuasion is an emotional as well as an intellectual activity, it comes from deep within the brain. When we agree with someone, we do so with our whole bodies. You can use this to drive agreement and create persuasion. Adopt a posture, and watch for others to adopt it. Once they have, change it slightly. If the others go along, you're well on your way to persuading the room.

Your control of the body language in the room will both create and test the strength of your persuasion (or lack thereof).

The reason is that people's bodies tell them what they're thinking, not the other way around. It's counterintuitive but true. Our minds basically say to ourselves, *I'm aligned physically with this person, so I must agree with her.* That's because we don't like to think of ourselves as acting with no reason.

You must use this control of the physical orientation of other people with sophistication and subtlety. It must be combined with a series of steps that include other kinds of consensus building. It won't work merely to come into a room, adopt a physical position, and expect everyone else to adopt your intellectual position too.

First, build agreement by adopting their positions, dealing with their concerns, and generally building on your openness to them and their openness to you. Do this work carefully while you're talking through the issues important to the situation. What you're doing is aligning your two conversations and using both of them to persuade the others in the room. It takes considerable practice to do this with subtlety and effectiveness, but once you master it, you'll find that your ability to persuade others will increase enormously.

Mirroring and basic body orientation must be adapted to the physical space and its constraints. If you are sitting facing someone whom you're trying to persuade, then your work on alignment will be limited to the head, the face, the shoulders, and the hands and arms. But that still leaves a whole retinue of possible behavior: bringing the hand up to the face in a thoughtful gesture, or bringing the arms and hands down out of view, for example, among many such possible moves.

When you're standing together, it's both easier and more powerful because you can involve the whole body. An amusing instance of this comes when you're speaking to a roomful of people, and someone starts giving you a hard time. Go over to that person and align yourself with him (literally, face the same way), within his personal space. Stand up while he is sitting down, and you'll find, because of the combination of authority and alignment, that the person will shut up immediately.

It takes a real psychopath to resist this treatment, and you won't run across those very often. Chances are very good that the person giving you a hard time only wants to be heard. When you create that alignment with the authority in the room, he's happy. Disagreement is oppositional, and you've just said to that person, without saying a word out loud, *We agree*. That's the power of the second conversation.

Once again, the unconscious mind knows all about alignment. We learn early on, in the cradle, when we watch parents (the ones who love and care for us) mimic our behavior, just as we learn to mimic theirs. Mother will tip her head so that it mirrors ours, and we'll coo madly at each other. That's where it all begins.

THE POWERFUL—SUBSERVIENT CONTINUUM

The story of power in a room is written in space and height.[7] It's not very different from what pack dogs do, in fact. Look for the alpha dog. He or she will be the highest person in the room if at all possible. It's why kings and queens have had thrones on daises since they began ruling others.

I used to ask CEOs I worked with to test this out by convening a meeting at a large conference table with the CEO highly visible in the middle. CEOs typically take the middle of the table, and sometimes the head, to express their power anyway.

Next, I instruct the CEO to sit tall in her seat at the start, but then to gradually sink down in the chair by sliding forward very slowly. The result? Those in the room who want to express their subservience to the CEO unconsciously sink lower and lower in order not to upstage the boss. CEOs have reported to me that they've barely been able to contain their amusement as they've watched everyone at the table slide slowly toward the floor.

A truly hilarious instance of this took place when Richard Branson, the Virgin companies tycoon, was giving a speech at a conference at Radio City Music Hall in Manhattan. Branson is not a comfortable or particularly good public speaker, so his clever staff had arranged for first a video, then a brief speech by Branson, and finally a question-and-answer session with a local TV personality in order to fill up the time as painlessly as possible for him.

When it came to the question-and-answer session, Branson, a genuine, unassuming man, sat in a relaxed way in his chair. The interviewer, not wishing to be higher than Branson, leaned forward with his elbows on his knees. Branson mirrored this behavior, but put his head a little lower than the interviewer's. Soon the two hapless public figures were crouched with their heads nearly between their knees, trying to carry on an intelligent conversation.

Finally, the interviewer could stand it no longer and stood up, saying to the audience, "Let's take some questions from you now." There was an audible groan of relief from the audience, who had been made uncomfortable by this ridiculous display of humility without consciously understanding what was going on. Neither did Branson or the interviewer.

Powerful people also take up more space: they splay their legs out, or their arms, or hog more space in the room. It's why important people get bigger hotel rooms than lesser folk, and it's why tall people are statistically more likely to rise higher in their professions than shorter people. The alpha dog strikes again.[8]

Powerful people employ a host of subtler signals of their dominance, from interrupting lesser mortals to talking more, to indulging in longer pauses. They make more eye contact, or less, depending on their choice. In fact, they dominate the eye contact and the physical touch—all the ballet of the second conversation. It's why it takes training to meet Queen Elizabeth, and when you leave, you have to back out of the room. All of that is simply to express her vast authority over the rest of us.

Powerful people may withdraw physically from a conversation, controlling its tempo and showing their power with this ability. I've seen people in a meeting lean back and put their hands behind their head in order to express their superiority over the rest of the room. It's arrogant but effective.

Power in nonverbal display is all about controlling your own behavior and that of others. Once again, this is something that your unconscious is exquisitely attuned to. You will immediately know when you are in the presence of someone who believes she is powerful because of all the signals I've described, as well as others, such as your own tendency to be obeisant in front of the person.

How do you take or project authority when you want to do it deliberately? Stand as tall as you can. Make sure you are the tallest person in the room if you can. Give yourself a taller chair if you're sitting by adjusting it to the maximum. Move less, and make people come to you. Don't mirror other people; let them mirror you. Have the window at your back if there is one. Control the distance between you and others. Don't let them in your space; rather, bring them in when it suits you.

President Lyndon Johnson was famous for using his height and physical closeness to dominate the people around him. He would bring his face within inches of others, violating their intimate space and making them supremely uncomfortable until they gave way.[9] It wasn't a particularly nice thing to do, but it was effective. Powerful people tend to dominate the conversation, or let a second in command take the conversation, and just listen.

There's a great story of Stanley, the famous explorer who found Livingstone, the missionary and explorer who wasn't lost himself but rather lost to Victorian England. Stanley was en route to finding Livingstone when he was captured by an unfriendly tribe of Africans. They took him to the village chief's house, a hut filled with fifty or so people. One of them, who was doing all the talking and seemed to be the most powerful person in the room, said, "If you can tell who is the chief, you live. If not, you die." Stanley studied the scene, then correctly pointed to a fifteen-year-old who was quietly sitting to one side. His life was spared. When asked later how he knew, Stanley said, "I looked for the one who was most like the Queen. The boy wasn't moving. He was the most powerful."[10] It was a brilliant early example of second conversation expertise.

THE COMMITTED—UNCOMMITTED CONTINUUM

When people are committed, they lean in to you.[11] They are open, sometimes subservient, always sincere, and allied. This last continuum is really a combination of the others, so the body language already described applies here.

It begins with the eyes: they're open, wide, and focused on you. The face is similarly open. Most of all, it will be close to yours. Closing the sale is all about closing the distance. It's why car sales reps constantly shake your hand. They're trying their hardest to build commitment, and they know that the mind follows the body.

The torso is open and closer to you than it is if not committed. There is no opposing chatter from the hands and arms, legs and feet. The person or persons may well be mirroring you if it's possible in the circumstances.

The act of commitment often is signaled with a change in body language, indicating a decision has been made. Look for it—the yea or nay. At that point, put your unconscious mind into high gear. Ask yourself, *Is this person committed?* You'll be able to tell very quickly if you see all the positive affect I've described—or its opposite.

Most of all, you'll feel comfortable. Commitment is a positive statement, and because we're social creatures, we humans like to achieve it. We're uncomfortable when it doesn't exist. So you can detect it by the general sense of comfort that you get when it happens. That's your unconscious telling you, *Yes, it's all good. They're going along with this!*

Commitment is a kind of connection, and one that makes us feel good. You'll know it when you see it. When it's not there, people express their discomfort with all sorts of agitation, discordant language, and attempts to leave. Of course, some cultures cover these awkward moments with an excess of agreement, positive body language, and superficial attempts at commitment. When Westerners first do business in Asia, they often find themselves misreading the Asian politeness and desire to save face for commitment. This is one instance when unconscious expertise lets them down.

OTHER CULTURES

While the basic rules of the second conversation are similar from one culture to another around the world, nonetheless there are key differences, and it pays to be sensitive to them. This is not the place for an extended discussion of cultural differences, but there are a number of excellent references on the subject.[12] It's best to take cultures on one by one, when you're going to visit another country, rather than trying to learn them all at once. Precisely because the body language we send out is deeply conditioned by our upbringing, when it isn't biological, it's hard to change.

Principles of
Persuasive Content

$$\equiv$$

The art of creating persuasive communications is traditionally known as *rhetoric*: "using language so as to persuade or influence others."[1] The ancient Greeks were the first masters of that art as the tradition has come down to us. It has been added to, refined, and corrupted over the centuries since then. It's time for a twenty-first-century update. The Greeks left some important things out, and communications styles have changed.

What they left out, most importantly, is a thorough, systematic theory of the second conversation, the nonverbal half of the equation. As you certainly know by now, we're typically only half-aware of what we're doing when we're communicating with other people, and it's not always the important half. In this chapter and the next, I'll combine the relevant research and ideas with my experience in order to create a modern, complete set of principles—an art of rhetoric, in the old-fashioned phrase—for both the verbal and the nonverbal conversations. These two chapters go into detail to help leaders understand what's at stake when they communicate in order to persuade. These are my rules for powerful communication, developed over twenty-two years of coaching, communicating, and writing. They sum up the previous chapters and set out my findings in the form of clear principles.

What happens when humans communicate? The best way to think about it, as I've argued, is as two conversations: the content and the nonverbal gesturing that occurs mostly without our conscious awareness.

There's a long tradition of writing about the content conversation, going back to the ancient Greeks.[2] The word *rhetoric* itself comes from the Greek word *rhetor*, a person hired in the public law courts of the time to argue on behalf of plaintiffs and defendants. So the Greeks pretty much invented lawyers, courts, and democracy, as well as a long tradition of judging people by their eloquence, a tradition that continues to this day.

At the same time, the Greeks also warned us against being deceived by mere words, giving us a cogent analysis of logical fallacies in public speech, all of which they used to great effect themselves, of course. They warned us, for example, of arguments ad hominem (the phrase is Latin, but the idea was Greek first), meaning "to the man," that is, arguments that are about a person rather than the relevance of his or her ideas. At the same time, they gave us a famous speech of assembled Greeks to Achilles, who was sulking, depressed, in his tent, rather than slaying Trojans, which was what the other Greeks wanted him to do. The rhetorical team flatters him egregiously, making a positive argument ad hominem that he was indispensable to the cause. The flattery worked, and Achilles went back to slaughtering Trojans, and Troy eventually fell.

We see these arguments today used endlessly in political debates, as candidates complain of another's flip-flopping on the issues as a reason not to elect that candidate rather than arguing the merits of one position or another. In fact, much of what passes for commentary or public debate today is argument ad hominem, especially during elections in the United States.

Thus, the rhetoric of persuasion has a long and colorful history, and we'll draw on that as we look at how to construct the art of the two conversations for leaders today.

Nonverbal conversation also has a long history of study, though not as thoroughgoing as the content. At least, we don't have as thorough a record of it. But people have been noting and decoding each other's gestures for thousands of years.

Several figures loom large among the Greeks and Romans: Aristotle, who developed a conceptual rhetorical framework; Demosthenes and the other law court speakers, who refined it in vigorous practice; and Cicero and Quintilian, the two great Roman theorists and practitioners who took the Greeks' foundation and built a timeless rhetorical edifice on it. Quintilian reports that Demosthenes, when he was asked what was the most important thing in the whole art of oratory, said it was delivery first, and delivery second, and delivery third, until finally they stopped asking him.[3] (Unfortunately, he didn't give us the details!)

Cicero set quite a high standard for effective speaking—a standard that surely most ancients didn't reach, and not many C-suite executives arrive at today either:

> In an orator, we must demand the subtlety of the
> logician, the thoughts of the philosopher, a diction
> almost poetic, a lawyer's memory, a tragedian's voice,
> and the bearing almost of the consummate actor.[4]

Cicero was a lawyer by training who eventually became a statesman and philosopher. He got the idea of the two conversations, writing as early as the 50s B.C.E. that "by action the body talks, so it is all the more necessary to make it agree with the thought."[5]

Quintilian too understood the importance of the two conversations. Here is what he said about it in the late first century C.E.:

> By far the greatest influence is exercised by the glance.
> For it is by this that we express supplication, threats,
> flattery, sorrow, joy, pride, or submission. It is on this
> that our audience hang, on this that they rivet their
> attention and their gaze, even before we begin to speak.
> It is this that inspires the hearer with affection or dislike,
> this that conveys a world of meaning and is often more
> eloquent than all our words.[6]

As a modern field of study, gesturing for effect first shows up in books for actors, who over the years have had to learn an increasingly subtle array of gestures that are calculated to evoke certain emotions in the minds of the audience.

Books from even 100 to 150 years ago seem ridiculously formalistic to us today, calculated to inspire laughter rather than the appropriate emotion, but in truth it is at least in part because they are so recognizable.[7] When an actor of the Victorian period recoiled, jaw slack, eyes wide open, palms open and facing forward, everyone at the time knew he was afraid. Today, we'd think, *How melodramatic*. But even today, our most lauded movie actors still open their mouths slightly and their eyes wide to indicate fear.

The point is that the conscious observation of unconscious gestures is an ancient study too. But what is far less common is the study of how these two conversations intertwine. It is scandalous that this is the case; communication is inextricably concerned with both, and one without the other is incomplete. More than that, the two must be taken together to understand the full communication: the all-important intent behind the words, for example, or the full force of the commitment being made. And to create an effective modern rhetoric for leaders, both conversations must be included. What's needed is a set of principles that links the verbal and the nonverbal together.

History is littered with people, leaders and otherwise, who have said one thing and meant another, who have used brave words to make a lukewarm commitment, who have lied with a straight face, or who have said no with their words and yes with their gestures. Indeed, it goes on everywhere around the world every day. That's not the news. What's odd is that there haven't been more thoroughgoing attempts to analyze these two intertwined conversations to see how they work together.

Why are we so aware of the verbal conversation and so unaware, most of the time, of the nonverbal? We use our muscles and brains to produce both, and we're responsible for both. Why do people, for example, consider it lying to lie with a straight face but not when the (partly conscious) gestures they use undercut the seriousness of the commitment they're making with their words? The example suggests the importance of the interplay of both conversations and the way in which gestures can trump content, especially when they're made conscious.

Leaders today must understand the ways in which the two conversations intertwine so that they can show up with charisma and authenticity and better evaluate others' communications. If for no other reason, YouTube and all the other information flows have made communication much more intimate, and thus far more likely to be about both conversations. Gone are the days when a leader was represented by a press release, a speech, a white paper, or even a distant figure behind a podium. It's now possible for virtually any member of the public to evaluate the communications of leaders in business, politics, education, and so on. This means that leadership must necessarily be concerned with communication in an immediate and personal way as never before. Mastery of the two conversations is not simply useful; it's essential. What are sensible ways to think about content, especially in unscripted communications? And how do you make content powerful, and persuasive? My rules for the road follow. Use them as they are helpful to you, and ignore them at your peril.

. . .

Rule 1: Persuasive rhetoric is about phrasing your arguments so that your listeners can hear them.[8]

Successful leaders understand this intuitively. They couch their arguments in their listeners' and audiences' terms as much as their own. Fundamentally, that means understanding the listeners' points of view before you try to persuade them. Does this sound obvious? Why then is it so rarely followed?

The failure to do this is the reason that extreme positions on either side of an argument are so off-putting for most of us somewhere in the middle of the debate. For example, it's hard for most people to listen to the extremes on either side of the abortion debate without thinking, *Why don't they make an effort to resolve the problem rather than just perpetuating it?* Most people (typically 60 to 70 percent in ongoing polling) think that abortion is not a good thing, but that it should be available to women as an option if they so choose. Yet to listen to either side of the debate is to hear people shouting past each other with no understanding of the other side's position. Rather than seeming eloquent, they come across as unreasonable.

Good communication begins with the psychology of the person or group you're communicating with. The Greeks understood this. You need to do this work first as a leader before you open your mouth to speak.

. . .

Rule 2: Persuasive rhetoric has a clear goal in mind and is usually transparent about it.[9]

The second mostly likely reason for good communications to turn bad is the lack of a clear goal. When you negotiate, you have a BATNA (the best alternative to a negotiated agreement): the minimum that you've decided you must achieve or you walk away. The same should be true in communications.

Is the meeting you're calling with an important client to do some specific business or just to keep the connection strong? Let the other party know, so that there are no broken hearts along the way. If the agenda hasn't been set beforehand, get agreement on it in the first few minutes of the meeting before hard feelings set in because of misunderstandings. The idea is to get straight in your own mind what you want to cover before you communicate. Then be open with your partner or partners.

Of course, there are times when prudence or tact, or both, demands that you be less transparent. In some high-stakes negotiations, it won't do to let the other side know your BATNA or even some lesser goals of the negotiations. There's merit in keeping secrets.

Similarly, in delicate communications between friends, lovers, spouses, and others with whom you are in close relationships, there are times when transparency is not kind or helpful. In the long run, though, the absence of transparency is fatal to any close relationship.

. . .

Rule 3: Persuasive rhetoric deals with problems and solutions.[10]

Think of a communication—whether a formal meeting, a one-on-one discussion about some issue the business faces, a speech, or a chance get-together in the hall—as a twofold exercise. The first step is to get agreement about a need, a problem, or an issue that you have in common. The second step is to explore solutions together. It's that simple: problem first, then solution. Thinking in these terms will help you structure your informal comments in conversations, meetings, and off-the-cuff remarks. You'll get a reputation as a clear thinker and a persuasive communicator if you follow this simple rule.

But too often people get impatient. They see the answer they want to achieve or support, and they jump to that point without taking their listener along with them. The result is resistance when they could have had agreement leading to action.

Here's the important point: you can't expect the other half of a communication to go along with you unless you take them on the same journey that you have taken (leading to a decision, a feeling, a point of view, an action). That means starting with the relevant inputs—the problem—and then finding a solution.

That doesn't necessarily mean taking them on the same historical journey that you went on. It's not always appropriate, and it's usually not interesting. Keep in mind that you must have the other communicators' perspectives in mind. What's important, interesting, and relevant to them in the journey that you want to take them on?

· · ·

Rule 4: Persuasive rhetoric deals in stories, facts, and tropes.[11]

These are your tools for building effective, emotionally convincing communications. Used properly—stories liberally, facts carefully, and tropes sparingly—they will give your communications life, zest, interest, and charisma. Failure to use them will result in communications no one else wants to listen to. We begin with stories.

We are awash in information, most of it random, and our attention spans and memories suffer accordingly. According to at least one theory, our minds develop by learning simple stories (when X does Y, Z happens), and we retain our facility for and love of stories for the rest of our lives.[12] Thus, your job as a communicator is to tell stories so that your listeners will hear you and remember what you've said. There are five basic stories in Western culture: the quest, the love story, the revenge story, the rags-to-riches story, and stranger in a strange land.[13] The first and most important is the quest. If you can suggest to your listener that you and she are on a quest together, the odds that she will enthusiastically join you rise greatly. We all understand and love quests.

You know the basic structure of a quest deep in your bones. A hero confronts a problem: the home is attacked by storm troopers, say, and Uncle and Auntie are killed. Off the hero goes to find something: himself, revenge, a way to stop the Evil Empire. Anyone who is a good guy is rooting for the success of the quest by this point. The hero runs across a mentor or teacher and learns some, but never all, of the life lessons he needs in order to proceed. Then the journey really begins, and the obstacles come at the hero left and right. After lots of adventures and the beginnings of wisdom, the hero eventually reaches the object of his quest and can celebrate, often by returning home, or at least partying with his new friends.

Most readers no doubt recognized both the general story line of that recitation and the specific tale: *Star Wars*. The good news is that you don't have to be going to Antui to tell a good quest story. The basic form is so sturdy and easily recognized that you only have to intone a few recognizable steps in the journey and everyone is ready to pack up and leave with you, enthusiastic recruits all.

And there's more good news. There are many situations in the business world that lend themselves easily to a good quest story. Business start-ups, new product launches, sales goals—indeed most of what businesspeople do—can all become quests.

The second most popular and effective story in our culture is the love story. And so well is it known that I don't need to describe it much, except to say that a good love story has three crucial stages. First, there's the meeting of the two people or things or cartoon characters destined to fall in love. It's either love at first sight or a slowly dawning awareness of love. Second, there's the falling out, when the party of the first part loses the party of the second part's affection because of accident, misunderstanding, or something dumb the guy did. Third, there's the healing of the rift. The lovers get back together, and everyone's happy.

How do you apply this venerable tale to your communications? Whenever it's about two people, or groups, or companies, or organizations, or nation-states getting together, it can be a love story. We all recognize this instinctively in the language we use to describe such linkages. We say the United States is "wooing" North Korea, for example, or the company "seduced" a new employee with great benefits, a high salary, and a really sexy car.

The power of love stories is so great in our culture that most of us throw ourselves enthusiastically into relationships of various kinds, assuming that they will play out like the three-part story, expecting life to follow our preprogrammed thinking. They are extraordinarily disappointed when they don't.

In the revenge story, the hero is wronged and usually suffers for most of the story trying to get a bit of his or her own back. Revenge, by killing, swindling, or ridiculing the enemy, usually comes after our hero has suffered a lot for a long time. Sophisticated revenge stories have a twist at the end, which involves the hero recognizing something in the villain—either a literal recognition or some sense that the two are alike in some way. These are dark matters, but we love good revenge stories because they help us believe that the world is in fact a just place despite nearly overwhelming, constant evidence to the contrary.

In a rags-to-riches story, the hero starts out poor; finds help along the way in the form of a magic bean, a flying carpet, or a rich uncle; and ends up rising to the occasion and the new style and driving a Porsche with the best of them. There's usually a large component of luck involved; the point of the story is almost always that the hero isn't special in any way—not especially intelligent or gifted or remarkable; rather, he or she is ordinary, in the sense of honest and true, like the rest of us.

You can use rags-to-riches stories in persuading people to join entrepreneurial ventures. These stories work well because the underlying message is that even ordinary people will win out. It's the triumph of the nerds, the unathletic, and the unremarkable.

Finally, my own favorite story is the stranger in a strange land. Here, a hero finds herself dropped into an unfamiliar terrain, or country, or place, and the goal is to make herself expert in the custom, land, or language in order to survive. This story is particular resonant today because of our sense that our world is changing so fast. New inventions, developments, and troubles bombard us. We are all strangers in a strange land in some way and to some extent. Every Monday morning is a new adventure.

The goal of this story is competence—the ability to cope with the unfamiliar. Many of us pride ourselves on our coping skills with new cultures, languages, technologies, or TV seasons. The story is widely applicable in business situations, political campaigns, and social change campaigns. Barack Obama used his own stranger in a strange land story extensively during his presidential campaign.

These stories are important in all kinds of communications because they are recognizable, they quickly enlist people to your point of view, and they carry a good deal of emotional freight with them. If you've told a good quest story and then look someone in the eyes, lower your voice, lean closer, and say, in husky tones, "So, will you help us?" she will be hard put to resist. It's simultaneously a personal and cultural call for help, and it's powerful.

Facts come a distant second to stories in our memory hall of fame. It's why President Reagan was deemed a great communicator and President Carter was not. Carter had the kind of mind that could retain facts, data, and specifics and didn't mind telling you about them. Reagan loved stories and couldn't remember facts. He had legions of index cards with stories for every occasion on them. And boy did he tell them! The result was that he was an effective leader (regardless what you think about his politics) where Carter was not (again, leaving politics aside for a moment).

That said, in communications with reasonable people, facts can be extraordinarily powerful if they are used carefully.

Sprinkle the conversation with a fact here or there, and you can clinch a deal, settle an argument, or end a debate. But I once heard a speaker (and he was speaking off the cuff) rise and say, "There are seventeen reasons as to why that approach won't work." Those of us in the audience held our collective breath while he ticked off the seventeen reasons. It was amazing; he got through all seventeen of them. Of course, none of us paid any attention to what he was actually saying. We were just listening spellbound to the numbers rolling by. And we had written him off as some sort of freak long before he got to the end. One or two telling facts can be powerfully persuasive. More facts are not. In fact, beyond a certain point (somewhere between two and seventeen, depending on the argument) more facts actually weaken an argument.

Tropes are the final arrow in your rhetorical quiver. They are the rhetorical devices that people notice most quickly, such as metaphors and similes.[14]

A little rhetoric goes a long way. If you use one metaphor or if you say, as President Kennedy did, "Ask not what your country can do for you, but what you can do for your country," the results can be profound. But there's a delicate line between that and rhetorical excess, which is immediately suspect in the average person's mind. William Safire wrote a line for Vice President Spiro Agnew to say to describe liberals: "nattering nabobs of negativism." It was a case of too much of a good thing—alliteration.[15]

If you extend the metaphor beyond a sentence or two, you will sound ridiculous. Or if you launch into a blizzard of syllepsis, synecdoche, and zeugma, even if your audience could not begin to identify the trope by its name, they would recognize that rhetoric was being practiced on them and react with derision or disdain, and never approval. Americans are a plain-speaking people on the whole, and a little rhetoric is like dessert after a big meal. A small taste might be just the thing to end things on a high note, but too much and the effect is ruined.

It's important to understand the power of tropes in framing and reframing a discussion. If a politician on the stump replies to an accusation by saying, "Well, that's the pot calling the kettle black," even as tired a cliché as that immediately puts the other party on the defensive because suddenly both candidates' misdeeds are on the table. The use of the metaphor in that situation turns the tables in the discussion.

It can be fascinating to watch a situation be transformed by the power of rhetoric. Is our business like the *Titanic*, and are we just rearranging the chairs on deck? Or are we navigating the perilous seas of competition to the safe harbor of innovation and profit? Which metaphor you subscribe to will determine how you feel emotionally about the discussion and how open you are to change, renewed effort, or new thinking. Listening closely to the metaphors that others use can give you a good reading on their emotional state and the extent to which they are optimistic or pessimistic about the situation.

· · ·

Rule 5: Persuasive rhetoric passes the test of four critical questions: Is it articulate? Is there a real alternative? Is the idea consequential? Do the words shock but not surprise?[16]

Is it articulate? When you're on the receiving end of rhetoric, listen closely for clarity. Articulateness is not only a virtue; it is also usually a sign of clarity of thought. The reverse is also true: if the communication isn't clear to you, it probably isn't clear to the sender. That's the time to demand rephrasing or to work with the communicator to figure out what's really being said.

Is there a real alternative? It's always useful to ask yourself, when someone is putting forth an idea, whether there's an alternative. If a politician says, for example, that he supports our troops, ask yourself, *What's the alternative?* Could a politician say, "I don't support the troops"? Obviously not. If that's the case, then there is no real idea behind the rhetoric. It's only grandstanding. This is a good test to apply to your own communications as well.

Is the idea consequential? Check the consequentiality of the idea. Does it amount to anything, or is it a tiny idea? Your time is valuable; don't waste it rearranging the deck chairs on the *Titanic.*

Does the idea shock but not surprise? A persuasive communication may shock us, but it shouldn't surprise us. Indeed, good communication does need to shock, because otherwise it won't get any attention in this information-saturated era. Beyond that, we should be able to recognize the fundamental truth of it. Things that are both shocking and surprising are truly rare. When Luke learns that Darth Vader is his father, the audience is shocked but not surprised. Some part of us recognizes that it's in some sense inevitable and logical. *Of course,* Darth Vader is Luke's father. That's why the Force is so strong within him.

In your own communications, feel free to shock people, but try not to surprise them in this sense of the word.

· · ·

Rule 6: Persuasive communication cuts through the clutter of information overload by dealing with safety issues.[17]

Turn Maslow's hierarchy of needs upside down in your mind. Maslow said that we take care of our needs in order, from the most basic to the more refined. So, we take care of physiological needs first—food and shelter, say—before we worry about love, esteem, or self-actualization. Maslow looked to a society where all our basic needs were taken care of and we could focus on self-actualization.

Nice, but we've got a ways to go. Until that halcyon day, imagine a hierarchy of communications as an inverted Maslow's hierarchy. Which would you pay attention to first: a communication about your personal safety, or one about the metaphorical meaning of hands in Dickens's *Great Expectations*? One certain way to get attention is to shout "Fire!" in a crowded theater.

To ensure that you're heard, you must figure out a way to make your communications about the safety of your audience in organizational (or business) terms. That's not as hard as it sounds. Most issues ultimately boil down to safety, or they're not worth worrying about.

The exception to this rule is the audience that has satisfied all the issues lower down on the hierarchy and can afford to pay attention to self-actualization. It's just not often you find such audiences. The billionaires' club, perhaps, is such an audience. And even then, if a safety issue arises, it will trump your lesser (because higher up the pyramid) concern.

· · ·

Rule 7: Authenticity and charisma in content require self-revelation in this confessional age.[18]

Being willing to confess something, even if it's small, is table stakes in this age, surrounded as we are by the no-holds-barred, tell-all, celebrity-infatuated media, which constantly dish up the most intimate details of the lives, real or imagined, of these people. Our culture is obsessed with being in the know, whether it's the inner workings of the West Wing, or the movie sound stage, or backstage with the stars. Secrets have shorter and shorter half-lives and higher and higher value until the moment they're revealed.

The safest leaders are the fully transparent ones, but of course leadership requires difficult choices in gray areas of the law, policy, and ethics, so the need for secrets has not gone away. They're just much harder to keep than they were even a decade ago.

One lesson that has been impossible for organizations to learn in spite of overwhelming evidence is that when a secret is discovered, the only possible response for a public entity is full disclosure. We have seen over and over again the perils of not coming clean. The cover-up inevitably leads to far worse damage than the initial revelation. And yet every organization caught in the media headlights seems determined to learn the lesson once again the hard way. If you're caught, confess. As painful as that is, it's much easier in the long run than the alternative.

Principles of Persuasive Nonverbal Communication

What about the nonverbal half of communication? What are the basics of a modern rhetoric of body language? This chapter continues the deep exploration of what it takes to fully control your communications as a leader in the twenty-first century. I have developed the following principles based on what the research and my findings show is effective.

. . .

Principle 1: When the verbal and the nonverbal are aligned, you can be an effective communicator. When they are not, your audience will believe the nonverbal every time.[1]

Albert Mehrabian made this observation at the beginning of modern research in communications. This testimony to the primacy of the nonverbal has been part of the research, and indeed part of our commonsense understanding of communication for many years, and yet the full implications of the relationship between the verbal and the nonverbal are only now beginning to be understood, thanks to the rapid progress in brain research.

The important implication of this insight, however, has not changed since Cicero held the senators in ancient Rome spellbound. Leaders need to develop keen self-understanding and self-control, or risk undercutting themselves when they communicate with their publics, their employees, their colleagues, and indeed their friends and family.

Consider a simple example. If a leader walks to the front of the room slowly and hesitantly, hunched over and looking down at the floor, and says to the waiting analysts, anxious to put the current lackluster numbers in perspective, "It's really great to be here today," in a monotone, then the game is already up. The analysts have begun to draw their own conclusions immediately. Some of them are already sending out "sell" orders on their BlackBerries.

In situations scripted and unscripted, leaders have to be able to align content and body language or risk undercutting their agenda and the future of their organizations. The stakes are that high. And yet simply stonewalling or lying about bad news is not going to be successful in the long run either. For one thing, most people are not good at it; they have revealing signals that give them away. For another, if you're caught in the public eye, and you will be eventually, then you've killed your credibility and authenticity with the world. Remember that there are no secrets for long in this era. Everything eventually becomes public.

By far the better route is as much transparency as you can muster. This approach has the added advantage of making it easier to square your content and your body language. At least you won't be trying to disguise a lie! But even if you're not lying, if you do not get control of your nonverbal communication, you will betray your message with nervousness, diffidence, or simple clumsiness, which in this hyperaware age looks like uncertainty—or worse.

People are not very good about making allowances for human frailty when it comes to leaders in the public eye. That's why rehearsal is so important. If you wing it, your body language will always betray that sense that you're making it up as you go along, because it is the first time you're undertaking that particular communication. You look like a neophyte, not a self-assured leader.

If you betray a little nervousness at the beginning of a presentation to Wall Street, the eagle-eyed denizens of that fabled place are not likely to say to themselves, "I'm seeing a little nervousness; that's natural under the circumstances. I'll wait to see how the discussion goes." Rather, the internal dialogue will go something like this: *Uh-oh. He looks nervous. I wonder what he's hiding? I'd better have a closer look at those numbers.* Why does it work that way? Because of the second important insight.

.   .   .

Principle 2: We interpret body language unconsciously in terms of intent.[2]

We always assume that the body language we see in others is meaningful and related to us and our presence. We have to, because of the way our brains are constructed. As I noted earlier, the reading of nonverbal communications happens in the limbic brain, and it happens faster than conscious thought. That system evolved to keep us alive in ancient times when quick reaction time was a matter of life and death. It remains true today, even though it is much less often a life-and-death issue. Today, if the boss stalks up the aisle past us, we immediately start guessing her state of mind. *What's up? Why is she angry? What did I do—or fail to do?* And so on.

You can notice yourself doing this simply by cataloguing your thoughts when you meet someone at the office or in the supermarket. Notice how quickly your mind starts developing scenarios involving the intent of the other person. It's automatic and preconscious thought. Those scenarios are the result of what your brain has already logged as essential information about your environment and the others in it.

· · ·

Principle 3: In the nexus between the verbal and the non-verbal conversations is persuasion, and that's concerned with leading someone else to make a decision. This is the essence of leadership communications.[3]

Leadership communications means, at its essence, persuasion. That's what leaders do, after all. They persuade people to work together and achieve more than they ever thought they could, reach apparently impossible goals, and put personal interest aside (at least temporarily) in favor of some larger group benefit.

Persuasion is changing someone else's mind. If the mind isn't changed, the person hasn't been persuaded. It's that simple. So the leader's job is to change minds. And thus at its heart, successful leadership always involves strong, clear communications. It's not a nice-to-have or a corollary. It's at the heart of leadership.

· · ·

Principle 4: Decision making is largely an emotional, and therefore a nonverbal, process.[4]

Putting persuasion (and therefore changing minds and decision making) squarely in the center of leadership means that an emotional process is central to what successful leadership does. More than that, it's a process that requires both intellectual finesse and nonverbal skill. A leader, in other words, has to be comfortable with argument and comfortable in his or her own skin. Self-awareness is critical to being successful here; understanding your own emotional journey and responses is essential if you're going to evoke and shape emotional responses in others.

Decision making is nine-tenths emotional and one-tenth intellectual justification. Most reasoning about decision making is ex post facto justification of a decision already made on emotional grounds. We decide to buy a house or a new car, for example, because we want it, or it feels right, or some other equally intangible reason. Then we collect intellectual reasons for the decision that we've already made in order to justify it to ourselves.

Advertising and marketing people know this to be true, of course, and they play on our emotions in all that they do. But they'd be better served taking us through the full decision-making process if they could, because then we'd stick to the product or service about which the decision was made. Ads and other marketing tricks that depend on a quick emotional response can just as quickly be cancelled out by the next ad that comes along. Real decisions, however, once made, have greater staying power.

. . .

Principle 5: The source of our nonverbal conversation is deep in the oldest part of the brain in emotions, survival, relationships, and the other fundamentals of human connection and our connection with our surroundings.[5]

Our gestures come out of a deep part of our brain, which is why they happen split seconds before the words that accompany them. We get the emotion or the need, or we sense the danger, and then we react. The conscious thought forms after that.

Thus, the second conversation is actually more primal than the first—the verbal one. It is less articulate but deals with more basic feeling than most of our verbal conversations. Gestures come from intent, emotional responses and needs, threats to our space, desires to connect with others we love, and so on.

We gesture to express our deepest human desires, needs, and feelings. That's why gestures are so powerful and why getting them right in a public communication leads to what we call authenticity, or charisma, or both, and getting them wrong does not.

Oddly enough, most of the work on gestures begins with the very few gestures we use that have coded meanings, like the infamous raised middle finger and Churchill's famous two fingers raised in a V for victory. As such, most modern approaches to gesture deal with the least important kinds and dismiss the rest as just the hand waving that accompanies speech.[6]

But this is to create a systemic approach based on the least important elements in the system. Instead, we need to realize the centrality and importance of hand waving and all the rest of emotionally meaningful gesture to communications, not push them to one side.

In fact, there's growing evidence that we perform some kinds of rational thinking first with our gestures and only second with our conscious, intellectual thought. To take a simple example, think about how you size up something to judge if it will fit into a container.[7] You do that sort of "thinking" with your body. You might express it by moving your hands in a squeezing gesture if it's going to be a close fit but you think it will work. Any language associated with this thinking would be secondary to the judgment made by your body first. This physical thinking, if you will, about essential human interactions with others and with our surroundings is emotional at root and core to how we make decisions, persuade others, and therefore lead.

· · ·

Principle 6: To become a persuasive communicator (and leader), you must first consciously master and then control your second conversation.

It's not much of a challenge for most of us to present ourselves as rational, reasonable people under situations where we're comfortable and not subjected to much stress. When the stakes are raised in a variety of ways, however, managing our rational selves becomes more difficult. Soon a smart observer will begin to notice leakage of all sorts of emotions around the edges of what we're attempting to communicate.

If we're in an important meeting, for example, and we sense that a decision is getting away from us or going in a direction that we don't like, most of us begin to betray signs of impatience, anger, anxiety, worry, even fear. Others to whom we're opposed in the meeting will read those signs unconsciously and perceive weakness because what they will read (correctly) is what we're signaling: we don't have control. This is analogous to the "tell" all poker players are said to have, revealing a strong or weak hand to the expert eye.

If we're to become effective leaders, we must first become aware of our emotional responses to these important situations and the gestures that go with the emotional responses. Then we must learn to control them. It's a two-step process because the source of these gestures, and most of the gestures themselves, are unconscious. We must proceed from unconscious expertise to conscious awareness, and finally to conscious expertise.

It's a tall order. First, it involves learning about and then controlling a complicated set of activities at the same time as we're talking. Second, there is the paradox that if we consciously control our gestures with our cerebral cortex, the gestures will follow our words rather than proceed them, and those around us will perceive them as inauthentic.

So how do we meet this challenge and control our gestures, thus becoming conscious experts, without becoming inauthentic? Principles 7 and 8 address this.

. . .

Principle 7: To *master* the second conversation, you must make yourself aware of your own unconscious behavior and that of others.

The first step is awareness: observation of your own physical gestures and their interplay with your verbal communications—and that of others as well. We all notice gestures when they are brought to our conscious attention for some reason; perhaps they are wrong for the occasion, or extreme, or ridiculous, or absurdly repetitive. But to become an effective leader, you have to look beyond the obvious and begin to note and catalogue the subtle code of behavior of yourself and everyone around you. This takes time and patience.

. . .

Principle 8: To *control* the second conversation, you must focus on your emotional intent rather than your conscious awareness.

The next step is to control your gestures so that you can align the nonverbal and the verbal effectively and persuasively. Here's where the paradox of conscious intent comes into play: if you think about this too much, you won't be able to do it. Instead, you have to focus on the underlying emotion you want to express, and let the gesture take care of itself.

There's good news in this, because emotions can be bigger, simpler, and slower to change than the verbal messages you're trying to convey. Before you go into a room for an important meeting, prepare yourself with the appropriate emotion—say, enthusiasm for a deal to be signed—and then shift it only as needed (say, if there is an unexpected roadblock). The paradox is to achieve control over your gestures by thinking not about them but about the intentions that drive them. If you think about the gestures themselves, they will happen too slowly and will look inauthentic. This is the real paradox that underlies the apparent one of being deliberately authentic.

The point is that what you are really doing is bringing to the conscious level your experience of your emotions and those around you. That's what it means to be fully present in the room.

. . .

Principle 9: To be perceived as an authentic public person, you must align your nonverbal and verbal conversations. This means aligning your emotional intent with your conscious thought.

If you master this emotional fluency, you learn to align the nonverbal and the verbal, and you will be perceived as authentic. That's the secret to leadership communications, and therefore leadership, today. It's about clarity of message, where message is now defined as containing both the intellectual and the emotional. Anything less won't work.

. . .

Principle 10: Authenticity and charisma derive from becoming open, connected, passionate, and listening with and to your audiences.

Beyond authenticity, presence and charisma come from developing this congruity of the verbal and the nonverbal through the four critical aspects of communicating with an audience of one or one thousand: openness, connection, passion, and listening. The last two steps especially contribute to presence and charisma. Each of these is a separate discipline, and they all have to be layered, one on top of the other, in order to achieve true charisma.

Without openness from you as the leader, your audiences won't allow you even to engage them. With openness, they will let you in. Without some effort at connection with your audiences, they won't hear you over the roar of the other messages they are getting constantly. With connection, you can cut through the information overload.

Without passion, you will fail to be remembered. With passion, you can make an impression. And without listening in this democratic age, audiences will reject you as ultimately not engaged with them. When you listen, you can achieve the kind of charisma and authenticity that will mark you as a rare leader, the kind that audiences will walk through fire to follow and support and for whom they will sacrifice gladly.

Conclusion

Leadership Is Communication

Mastering communications of all sorts means mastering the two conversations, the verbal and the nonverbal. The purpose of this book is to help leaders learn to become persuasive communicators. It shows them how to structure their verbal conversations and bring to consciousness their nonverbal conversation and awareness of the nonverbal conversations of others.

CONTROL YOUR BODY LANGUAGE BY CONTROLLING YOUR INTENT

Once you've become a conscious master of the nonverbal conversation, you can learn to control it effectively by dealing with it in the realm of intent. That is, rather than trying to control every gesture consciously or notice and decode every gesture of the others you communicate with, you can instead decide on the intent, the emotion, the objective of the communication. If you focus on that strongly, you will find that your gestures will naturally follow your intent, your two conversations will be aligned, and you can become a powerful communicator. And you will become much more astute at reading others' intent in their body language.

Most of us assume that we are primarily conscious beings with an intellect that plans, weighs objectives and options, and directs action—like having a movie director sitting in our head. But in fact, as recent research and my work with clients shows, we are far more interesting and complicated beings than that. Our unconscious thought processes are far more sophisticated and influential than we have previously acknowledged. Instead of rational beings driven consciously by ideas, we are both conscious and unconscious beings driven by ideas and needs, plans and fears, thoughts and subconscious calculations that often happen in the blink of an eye before we can be aware of them.

We seek safety, we judge others, we duck incoming missiles, we analyze our surroundings, we give reassuring hugs, we make instant decisions about our feelings and how others are going to behave toward us. All of that is going on under the surface, faster than we can think consciously. It is only afterward that we come up with conscious rationales for what our subconscious minds have already decided for us.

This means that a good deal of the important work of being a leader—creating strong bonds with followers and colleagues, evaluating the mental states of people around us, persuading others to share a vision that we can see but others cannot—takes place at the unconscious and conscious levels simultaneously. Leaders who ignore the former and focus only on the latter ultimately will be halfway leaders—and not the most important half at that.

Are strong communication skills essential for successful leadership? In many ways, leadership *is* communications, since leaders are defined by their followers, and you can't create, inspire, and direct followers without communicating with them.

A leader who is a strong communicator has a chance to be successful through his or her followers. A weak communicator has no chance at all.

WATCH OUT FOR ROADBLOCKS TO ALIGNING THE VERBAL AND NONVERBAL

I've mentioned alignment of the nonverbal and the verbal throughout this book and note that it is essential for effective communications and thus effective leadership. Be aware, though, of roadblocks on the way to this alignment of conversations. Leaders who are not aware of their second conversations take their chances on success or failure. If by some happy chance, their words and their second conversation align, then it all works. If not, everyone in the room senses that something is missing.

Leaders who are not in control of their second conversations similarly risk ineffectiveness. I once saw the magic act of Penn and Teller, two accomplished showmen: Penn is the talkative one, and Teller is largely silent. Penn keeps up a running commentary designed to distract and bemuse the audience while they both perform the magic tricks. I was astonished to see that the talkative one, Penn, had a bad case of "happy feet": he had so much energy that he was wandering all over the stage randomly while chattering away. The random movement of his feet was his method for discharging that adrenaline-induced energy.

The result was so distracting, though, that I found myself unable to attend to his patter or even the magic tricks with any reliability. Nonetheless, he managed to hold his audience reasonably well until an unpleasant trick that involved apparently putting a live rabbit through a wood chipper. He lost his audience then and never got it back, making it clear that the bond was weak throughout, partly because his motion was random and not purposeful, toward the audience and away from it.

It's impossible to believe that a successful professional like Penn was not aware of his motion around the stage. I'm forced to conclude that he was simply unable to control it, and that lack of control was fatal for the success of the show. Indeed, he was even heckled by one or two audience members and approached by at least one after the show, who gave him a lecture on the mistreatment of animals. Because he had not related effectively to the audience, thus building trust, when the moment of truth came, the audience didn't believe him.

USE YOUR ADRENALINE

Fear is another reason that leaders fail to control and align their two conversations adequately. It is worthwhile saying a little more about fear and how to assuage it. For most of us (some 80 percent of the population), the fear we experience during some kinds of communications, such as important meetings, speeches, and other more public communications, is adrenaline based. That means that it's unpleasant but not debilitating. With a little work, we can turn it to our advantage.

How do you use adrenaline to help you in important communications? The first thing to understand is that it is your body's way of preparing you for crucial moments such as chasing down woolly mammoths and saber-toothed tigers. Today, giving speeches seems to have taken the place of the mammoth and the tiger. Nonetheless, your body is still preparing you, so your brain works a little faster, your heart pumps a little harder, you stand a little straighter, and therefore you're readier than you otherwise would be. In fact, you're more like the leader you aspire to be.

The problem is that the physical sensations are unpleasant when they don't lead to much in the way of physical action. Running after a tiger, or from one, is a great way to discharge excess physical energy. Standing in front of an audience is not. But instead of dancing around like a puppet minus the strings or like Penn, you should focus on those annoying physical symptoms and redefine them as the signs of the good energy that they are. Tell yourself, *My hands are clammy, my heart is beating fast, and my mind is racing. I'm ready to run with the mammoths and tigers! This is what I need to do a good job!*

If you work on this each time you experience the sensations, you'll learn to respect, value, and even enjoy the symptoms of adrenaline. I used to tell my college students, "Your heart is racing, your cheeks are flushed, your mind is in overdrive, your hands are clammy. What is about to happen?" I could always count on one or two cheeky youths to shout out, "Have sex!" which made the point perfectly for them.

The other thing you can do before an important meeting is focus on your offstage beat and breathe. Both activities will distract you and lead to a discharge of the adrenaline. If you're feeling twitchy, go for a walk or take some other form of gentle exercise. Don't overdo it. You don't want this to work too well and wear you out, so make sure that you've always got a little adrenaline at important moments for the boost it will give your brain.

WHAT TO DO IF IT'S REALLY STRESSFUL

What about the 10 percent of the population that is terrified about communicating to more than a handful of people at a time? How can they deal with the excess of adrenaline that they experience, which can be completely debilitating. I've worked with many executives who were paralyzed with fear at the thought of chairing an important meeting or giving a presentation.

If the standard methods I've just outlined are not enough to enable you to cope with your jitters, it's time to put your unconscious to work.[1]

Remember that your unconscious is the arbiter of many of your emotions and intent: it's driving your fear. It believes that you're in danger and is sending you the appropriate signals to help you escape from it. You have to retrain it to recognize the meeting or the speech as a wonderful opportunity for good things, not a potential disaster.

To do that, you have to talk to it and bridge the divide between conscious and unconscious. The method is surprisingly simple. Decide what is causing you the fear, and say it as clearly as possible to yourself. For example, you might say something like, *I become afraid when I think that the eyes of everyone in the room are on me, and I have to say something*. Or, *I become afraid when everyone expects me to know what to do*.

Now imagine the opposite, positive feeling: *It's thrilling to be the one everyone looks to to say something intelligent*. Or, *I'm happy that everyone expects me to know what to do*. Then take that thought and turn it into a rule, a constant state: *I always have something intelligent to say.* Or, *I always know just what to do. I'm cool.*

You must say this over and over again to yourself at downtimes throughout the day. Most of all, you need to repeat this like a mantra when you're falling asleep, when you wake up in the middle of the night, and whenever you get the negative thought or feeling that created the problem.

If you carry this out diligently, you'll find that your fear has disappeared within a few weeks. This is one time that it pays to be an insomniac. If you're awake for hours in the night, spend those hours repeating your mantra to yourself, and you'll make even more rapid progress.

That half-asleep, half-awake state is key, because your conscious mind and your unconscious mind seem to have more connection then. That's why it's so important to say your positive statement over and over to yourself when you're in that twilight space between sleeping and waking. If your mind starts arguing with you, just patiently keeping saying the rule: *I always know just what to do. I'm cool.*

For this technique to work, you have to be honest with yourself. You must accurately confront and label what's frightening you. If you don't label it clearly, you'll conquer some other fear that you don't have and miss the one that matters.

NEVER BE AFRAID AGAIN

Never give your unconscious negative thoughts or positive ones stated negatively, like *I won't be afraid.* Your unconscious will hear only the word *afraid,* and you'll terrify yourself. That's what you've done all these years to get yourself into a state of fear.

Once you've mastered your worst fears, you can use the technique to improve your communication skills generally. Let's say you have a tendency to ramble when speaking off the cuff in meetings. Give yourself mantras like, *I am a clear and persuasive communicator*. Whatever areas you would like to improve in, state those as positive attainments, and add them to your list.

Of course, you'll improve only to the extent that you understand what "clear and persuasive" means. It never hurts to seek objective evaluation and education so that you can raise your sights. What this work will do is lessen the likelihood that you will undercut yourself or betray yourself with a fear-based thought or action at the wrong moment.

This technique is a modified form of the mental imaging that seems to have begun with Russian Olympic athletes and spread around the world, first in competitive athletic circles and then to the general population. It works for winning the gold medal because it prevents the mind from getting in the way. And it will work for your more stressful kinds and moments of communication.

Think for a minute about the negative thoughts that are lodged in your unconscious. From childhood fears to adolescent angst to the pressures of adulthood: it's all marinating in your mind, just out of reach of your conscious thoughts—all the times when someone said, *You're not smart enough, not fast enough, not good enough, not the right person, not the one I want.* But it is close enough to make you react with tension, a memory lapse, a knee-jerk negative reaction, or an irrational fear at just the wrong moment—a moment when you're called on to be great and act from your best self, not your worst. Why not spend some time molding some positive thinking in your unconscious? It will serve you very well at precisely the times when you need it most.

WE HUMANS HAVE TO GET ON THE SAME WAVELENGTH

Sociologists Stanford Gregory and Stephen Webster of Kent State University conducted some fascinating research into the question of leadership at a very simple level.[2] They studied interviews on the *Larry King Live* show and tapes of British politicians and former U.S. presidents. Why this particular grouping of people? Because the issue of power and deference is bound to come up when high-status individuals are involved.

What they studied were the low-frequency sounds (below 500 hertz) that we all utter as we speak. The existence of the sounds themselves was well known to researchers but had been dismissed as irrelevant. Gregory and Webster found that in conversations and meetings, people rapidly match each other's low-frequency sounds. In order to have a productive conversation or meeting, we need to literally be on the same wavelength.

It gets more interesting: the researchers found that lower-status people match the higher-status people in the room. You might expect that everyone would meet in the middle, but that was not the case. When Larry King was interviewing someone of very high status, he matched the high-status individual's tones. When the interviewee was low status, he or she would match Larry King. The quickest to match Larry was Dan Quayle, presumably someone who had good reason to be deferential.

What's going on here? Sorting out who is the most powerful person in the room is an important game that humans have used for time out of memory because relative status is important to us. This need to defer and assert probably goes back to more primitive times when our lives depended on it. Now it's more likely to be important when picking sides for a sports team, jockeying for power in a business meeting, negotiation, or perhaps picking a new pope.

The point is that there is an unconscious element to it that is literally beyond our ken. Which happens first? And what are the criteria? Gregory and Webster's research indicates that the process happens quickly, in the first few minutes of the conversation. So it's hardly the case that much conscious thought has gone into determining who should be top dog. Rather, once again we see that an important part of our relationships to others is determined, at least in part, unconsciously. We are not the rational beings we like to think we are. In this case, we don't even know what the criteria for selection are.

Conscious awareness of this unconscious process will arm you to resist the powerful and increase your own power. Just like the unconscious work of conquering your fears, awareness of this tendency to align around the powerful is key to navigating the leadership seas.

WHY WE GESTURE

Another way to come at this idea of the interplay between unconscious and conscious is to ask why we gesture at all. If you imagine that you can communicate effectively with your words alone, why waste the energy? Why is all this unconscious effort going on? Yet people who are blind from birth gesture.[3] All of us gesture more when we have listeners, and even more when we have viewers. We gesture most of all when we're having a hard time getting our point across. Bilingual speakers gesture more in their weaker language. The more options you have in a conversation, the more you gesture. The more complicated the task is, the more you gesture. Most of us have caught ourselves on the telephone gesturing, even as we realize that the other person can't possibly see us. Still, we keep gesturing. So it must help in some way, or we wouldn't keep doing it. Right?

Susan Goldin-Meadow, a researcher into learning effectiveness, has discovered that people learn faster when they're allowed to gesture than when they're not.[4] There must be some advantage that it confers. Her theory is that it reduces cognitive load, but given what we now know about mirror neurons, it seems likely to me that gesturing is simply trying stuff out—the evidence of something going on faster and deeper in the brain that the conscious frontal lobe can report or verbalize. And that may give us a real clue as to why I say that the second conversation is so important to communication. Goldin-Meadow did a clever bit of research in which she demonstrated that when someone is told a story and given information that is contained only in gestures, the person picks up the ideas and can recreate them in speech and gesture.

For Goldin-Meadow, the big "aha" is that mismatches between speech and gesture go up when someone doesn't know the correct answer or procedure. More than that, it is possible to know something at the level of gestures that you don't know verbally. Gesture, suggests Goldin-Meadow, is the place for learning, for experimentation, for being open to new ideas.

WHY DO WE TALK, THEN?

Perhaps the question should not be, "Why do we gesture," but rather, "Why do we talk?" The second conversation is the primal one in many ways. It is far more powerful in conveying many of the interconnections between humans that we find most important. Which means more to you at a crucial moment: a hug or a comment, even a nice one?

As a culture, we have a bias toward the word, but words are linear, whereas gesture is multidimensional. Gestures have many more meanings than words typically do. And at the same time, gesture can even be more precise than language. If you say, "I climbed the stairs" while gesturing a spiral staircase, we learn something through your hands that we didn't through your words.

For years, researchers and writers on the subject of gesture have begun with specific gestures that signal some particular thought, like circling your finger and thumb when you mean "okay." Much of the work by Desmond Morris and many others has been about cataloguing these gestures and their variations around the world.[5] Hilarity ensues when a gesture that means "nothing" in one culture is obscene in another. Thus, researchers have tended to dismiss the gestures that accompany speech as irrelevant or too messy and complicated to deal with. And their theories have similarly slighted these gestures as not important but rather mere meaningless accompaniments to speech.

You should now see clearly that the traditional approach to speech and gesture has got it exactly backward. It makes more sense to say that speech accompanies gesture. At all the really crucial moments and for the really important things, gestures speak louder than words. Emotions are expressed first and most powerfully in gesture, if only in a tear. Power, as I've just shown, is evaluated, measured, sorted out, and expressed in gesture long before it is in speech. In fact, a good deal of speech serves to smooth over naked aggression. Very young children simply grab each other's toys, but as they grow older, they develop elaborate verbal explanations and justifications for borrowing them.[6]

Connection between people is constantly expressed physically in gesture, orientation, closeness, openness, and other ways, even when it is concealed in language. Similarly, relationships are most directly expressed in gesture and in physical ways.

Reinforcement, contradiction, commentary, and so on are expressed primarily, or at least first, in gesture. We nod vigorously, shake our heads, and roll our eyes, and all of that expresses our reactions more powerfully and immediately than words can. The list goes on: duration, time, movement, action, spatial relationships, and pointing are all based in gesture.

GESTURES COME FIRST

Gestures suggest what a person will move to next in thinking. One study showed that gesturing in a circular motion made it more likely that a person telling a story would tell a circular story.[7] When people gesture without using speech, their gestures take on more of the characteristics of language; they become more ordered, linear, and numerical, for instance.

The point is that gestures are powerful, holistic, emotional, vague, and flexible—not because that's all they can do, but because they do those things best, and they are a separate and vital part of communication. The most widely used gestures around the world are the head shake for no; the head nod for yes; the shoulder shrug, meaning "I don't know"; the hand on one cheek while tilting the head for sleep; the palm held up at waist height with wiggling fingers to indicate "come here"; and the palm facing out at chest height to indicate "stop."

But those are merely the most universal ones, not necessarily the most expressive or the most powerful. Anthropologist David Givens, director of the Center for Nonverbal Studies in Spokane, Washington, researches gestures like the palms-up gesture, which has a variety of meanings around the world but mostly seems to be asking for something. If you shrug your shoulders at the same time, you mean, "It's not my fault," or, "How could I know?" Givens's theory is that the gesture is a by-product of the instinctive submission gesture in animals from eons ago.[8]

I would rather note how open it makes you feel when you try it. When you open your arms out to people, at a level just above the waist, with your palms facing upward, you are saying, in effect, "Trust me; I'm open to you." The really interesting result of that gesture is that your thoughts open up too. You find yourself speaking more frankly and fully than if you have your arms crossed. The second conversation is really the first one. Gestures drive thoughts, not the other way around.

GRASP THE IMPORTANCE OF
BOTH CONVERSATIONS

The effect of gesturing openness is to allow a relationship to begin. The second conversation is really the first one.

Nonverbal communication has been ignored by leaders for far too long or treated as an accompaniment to speech. So they spend enormous amounts of time and effort getting their words right. Lawyers are paid millions to make sure that the words are not actionable. And yet the real conversation is happening all the time around them, and it's a conversation that they're only dimly aware of.

Don't make that mistake. Grasp fully the importance of both conversations. Leaders must learn the language of gesture just as they learn the verbal one. And they must clarify their intent in important one-on-one chats, meetings, speeches, and negotiations, so that their two conversations work together to make powerful, persuasive communications.

Every communication is two conversations. Leaders can't afford to speak with diffidence, ambivalence, or confusion for long. If their nonverbal conversation reveals their uncertainty, that feeling will quickly spread to everyone around them.

Leaders over the years have confessed after the fact to doubts about some important decisions, doubts that they were able to conceal at the time. Churchill, for example, knew many nights of indecision, uncertainty, and anguish during World War II, yet he was careful not to let that show during his radio broadcasts and speeches to the House of Commons. How fortunate for England that it had a leader who was able to radiate confidence even during that country's darkest hours![9]

The art of persuasion depends on consistency in message from both conversations. That means successful leaders have to learn how to control and align the two when it counts. Lives may literally depend on that control.

You now have the tools you need to manage your communications consistently. You have work ahead of you to do because it's harder to think about both conversations at the same time than it is to think only about your content. But it's the price of effective leadership, and the reward is powerful, persuasive communication.

Notes

INTRODUCTION

1. For an excellent description of the mysteries of the brain, and in particular a discussion of how the brain signals motion before we're consciously aware of it, see the oddly mistitled *A General Theory of Love*, by T. Lewis, F. Amini, and R. Lannon (New York: Random House, 2000), especially Chapter Two. Despite the title, this is a serious book about human psychology and biology written by three doctors.

CHAPTER ONE

1. T. Lewis, F. Amini, and R. Lannon, *A General Theory of Love* (New York: Random House, 2000), especially Chapter Two.

2. Albert Mehrabian's work is seminal. See his *Silent Messages: Implicit Communication of Emotions and Attitudes*, 2nd ed. (Florence, Ky.: Wadsworth, 1981). See also A. Mehrabian and S. R. Ferris, "Inference of Attitudes from Nonverbal Communications in Two Channels," *Journal of Counseling Psychology*, 1967, *31*, 248–252; A. Mehrabian and M. Wiener, "Decoding of Inconsistent Communication," *Journal of Personality and Social Psychology*, *6*, 1967, 109–114; and A. Mehrabian and M. Williams, "Nonverbal Concomitants of Perceived and Intended Persuasiveness," *Journal of Personality and Social Psychology*, 1969, *13*, 37–58.

3. *The New Shorter Oxford English Dictionary* (New York: Oxford University Press, 1993), p. 375.

4. N. Morgan, *Working the Room: How to Move People to Action Through Audience-Centered Speaking* (Boston: Harvard Business School Press, 2003), reprinted as *Give Your Speech, Change the*

World: How to Move Your Audience to Action (Boston: Harvard Business School Press, 2005).

CHAPTER TWO

1. See A. Mehrabian, *Silent Messages: Implicit Communication of Emotions and Attitudes*, 2nd ed. (Florence, Ky.: Wadsworth, 1981), Chapter Five.

2. C. Stanislavski, *An Actor Prepares* (New York: Theatre Arts, 1987).

3. M. McLuhan and Q. Fiore, *The Medium Is the Message* (New York: Random House, 1967).

CHAPTER THREE

1. "1982 Chicago Tylenol Murders," retrieved Apr. 2008 from http://en.wikipedia.org/wiki/1982_Chicago_Tylenol_murders.

CHAPTER FOUR

1. P. Ekman, *Telling Lies: Clues to Deceit in the Marketplace, Politics, and Marriage* (New York: Norton, 1985), especially Chapters 3–5.

2. The universal facial gestures that Darwin first noted are described in Ekman, *Telling Lies*, and D. McNeill, *The Face* (New York: Little, Brown, 1998).

3. Mehrabian, *Silent Messages: Implicit Communication of Emotions and Attitudes*, 2nd ed. (Florence, Ky.: Wadsworth, 1981).

4. Ekman, *Telling Lies*.

CHAPTER FIVE

1. Kennedy's *Ich bin ein Berliner* speech can be found in full in William Safire's wonderful book, *Lend Me Your Ears: Great Speeches in History* (New York: Norton, 1992), pp. 493–495.

2. A. C. Kinsey, W. B. Pomeroy, and C. E. Martin, *Sexual Behavior in the Human Male* (Philadelphia: Saunders, 1948). A. C. Kinsey, W. B. Pomeroy, C. E. Martin, and P. Gebhard, *Sexual Behavior in the Human Female* (Philadelphia: Saunders, 1953).

3. Cited in D. Cannadine (ed.), *Blood, Toil, Tears and Sweat: The Speeches of Winston Churchill* (Boston: Houghton Mifflin, 1989), pp. 148–149.

4. B. Clinton, *My Life* (New York: Knopf, 2004), p. 9.

5. Jack Germond, *Fat Man in a Middle Seat: Forty Years of Covering Politics* (New York: Random House, 1999), p. 11.

6. The reciprocity rule comes originally from R. B. Cialdini's great book, *Influence: Science and Practice* (Needham Heights, Mass.: Allyn & Bacon, 2001).

7. Cialdini, *Influence*.

8. Cialdini, *Influence*.

9. M. Gladwell, *The Tipping Point* (New York: Little, Brown, 2000).

10. Cialdini, *Influence*.

11. Churchill's "finest hour" speech can be found in full in Cannadine, *Blood, Toil, Tears and Sweat*, pp. 166–178.

12. Cialdini, *Influence*.

13. Gladwell, *Tipping Point*, p. 30.

CHAPTER SIX

1. A. Mehrabian, *Silent Messages: Implicit Communication of Emotions and Attitudes*, 2nd ed. (Florence, Ky.: Wadsworth, 1981), pp. 13ff. The four zones are described in many books on nonverbal communications, based on the work of anthropologist Edward T. Hall. See, for example, M. L. Knapp and J. A. Hall, *Nonverbal Communication in Human Interaction* (Orlando, Fla.: Harcourt, 1997). For the postures, see, for example, V. P. Richmond and J. C. McCroskey, *Nonverbal Behavior in Interpersonal Relations* (Needham Heights, Mass.: Allyn & Bacon, 2000). I have taken the general research into the meaning of posture and codified it into the three described in the chapter in order to make it easy to discuss and understand.

CHAPTER SEVEN

1. Senator Barack Obama's speech on Reverend Jeremiah Wright is quoted in full on his Web site, http://www.barackobama.com.

2. N. Maclean, *A River Runs Through It* (Chicago: University of Chicago Press, 1976), p. 159.

3. King's speech can be found in full in W. Safire, *Lend Me Your Ears: Great Speeches in History* (New York: Norton, 1992), pp. 495–500.

4. The tropes from ancient Greece can be found in E. Corbett and R. Connors, *Classical Rhetoric for the Modern Student* (New York: Oxford University Press, 1999), Chapter Four.

5. President Kennedy's inaugural address can be found in Safire, *Lend Me Your Ears*, pp. 811–814.

CHAPTER EIGHT

1. The best source for wisdom on the voice is P. Rodenburg, *The Right to Speak: Working with the Voice* (New York: Routledge, 1992). Other sources for this material include the authoritative work, E. Skinner, *Speak with Distinction* (New York: Applause, 1990); R. Grant-Williams, *Voice Power: Using Your Voice to Captivate, Persuade, and Command Attention* (New York: Amacom, 2002); C. Jones, *Make Your Voice Heard: An Actor's Guide to Increased Dramatic Range Through Vocal Training* (Washington, D.C.: Back Stage Books, 1996); C. Berry, *Your Voice and How to Use It: The Classic Guide to Speaking with Confidence* (New York: Virgin, 1994); and D. G. Davies and A. F. Jahn, *Care of the Professional Voice: A Guide to Voice Management for Singers, Actors and Professional Voice Users* (London: A&C Black, 2004).

CHAPTER NINE

1. I have been unable to locate the original source of this taxonomy of listening. If any can be provided, I would be happy to credit it properly in a subsequent edition.

2. Thanks to Kathleen Smith.

CHAPTER TEN

1. M. Gladwell, *Blink: The Power of Thinking Without Thinking* (New York: Little, Brown, 2005), pp. 3–5.

CHAPTER ELEVEN

1. This schema has evolved from the one that I introduced in *Working the Room*, based on work with clients since 2003. N. Morgan, *Working the Room: How to Move People to Action Through Audience-Centered Speaking* (Boston: Harvard Business School Press, 2003), reprinted as *Give Your Speech, Change the World: How to Move Your Audience to Action* (Boston: Harvard Business School Press, 2005).

2. Bill Clinton's grand jury testimony as widely reported in the news; see, for example, the BBC's "Review of the Year 1998," Dec. 22, 1998.

3. See "Pheromones," retrieved Apr. 2008 from http://en.wikipedia.org/wiki/Pheromones.

4. P. Ekman, *Telling Lies: Clues to Deceit in the Marketplace, Politics, and Marriage* (New York: Norton, 1985).

5. Ekman, *Telling Lies*. The training DVD is available at http://www.mettonline.com/products.aspx.

6. The schema is mine. For the basic body language research, see M. L. Knapp and J. A. Hall, *Nonverbal Communication in Human Interaction* (Orlando, Fla.: Harcourt, 1997), and V. P. Richmond and J. C. McCroskey, *Nonverbal Behavior in Interpersonal Relations* (Needham Heights, Mass.: Allyn & Bacon, 2000).

7. Once again, the schema is mine; the basic body language research is widely available. Knapp and Hall, *Nonverbal Communication in Human Interaction*, and Richmond and McCroskey, *Nonverbal Behavior in Interpersonal Relations*, have good summaries.

8. The research into the effects of height is widely available. See, for example, L. Malandro, L. Barker, and D. A. Barker, *Nonverbal Communication* (New York: McGraw-Hill, 1989).

9. See R. Goodwin *Remembering America: A Voice from the Sixties* (New York: Little, Brown, 1988).

10. The story is in T. Jeal, *Stanley: The Impossible Life of Africa's Greatest Explorer* (New Haven, Conn.: Yale University Press, 2007).

11. The schema is mine; the basic body language research is widely available. For example, see Knapp and Hall, *Nonverbal Communication in Human Interaction*, and Richmond and McCroskey, *Nonverbal Behavior in Interpersonal Relations*.

12. See R. E. Axtell, *Gestures: The Do's and Taboos of Body Language Around the World* (Hoboken, N.J.: Wiley, 1998); F. L. Acuff, *How to Negotiate Anything with Anyone Anywhere Around the World* (New York: Amacom, 1997); and T. Morrison and W. A. Conaway, *Kiss, Bow, or Shake Hands* (Cincinnati, Ohio: Adams Media, 2006).

CHAPTER TWELVE

1. *The New Shorter Oxford English Dictionary* (New York: Oxford University Press, 1993) defines *rhetoric* as "the art of using language so as to persuade or influence others; the body of rules to be observed by a speaker or writer in order to achieve effective or eloquent expression" (p. 2587).

2. See E.P.G. Corbett and R. J. Connors, *Classical Rhetoric for the Modern Student*, 4th ed. (New York: Oxford University Press, 1999), for a discussion of the rhetoric of the ancient Greeks, especially Chapters Three and Four.

3. Quintilian, *Institutio Oratoria*, XI.iii.6.

4. Cicero, *De oratore* I.xxviii.128.

5. Cicero, *De oratore* III.lix.222.

6. Quintilian, *Institutio Oratoria*, XI.iii.72.

7. For an amusing example of this sort of instruction, see D. Hoffman, *How to Be an Absolutely Smashing Public Speaker Without Saying Anything* (New York: American Heritage Press, 1970).

8. Phrasing in terms your listener favors is an idea that goes back to the Greeks. This particular expression of the principle is mine. See Corbett and Connors, *Classical Rhetoric for the Modern Student*, especially Chapters One and Two.

9. Being clear about communications goals is an old idea; the formulation here is mine.

10. For the problem-solution structure, see H. Ryan, *Classical Communication for the Contemporary Communicator* (Palo Alto, Calif.: Mayfield Publishing, 1992), especially Chapter Three.

11. Corbett and Connors, *Classical Rhetoric*, Chapter Four.

12. M. Turner, *The Literary Mind* (New York: Oxford University Press, 1996).

13. N. Morgan, *Working the Room: How to Move People to Action Through Audience-Centered Speaking* (Boston: Harvard Business School Press, 2003), reprinted as *Give Your Speech, Change the World: How to Move Your Audience to Action* (Boston: Harvard Business School Press, 2005), Chapter 6.

14. Among other tropes are antanaclasis, anthimeria, apostrophe, auxesis, erotema, hyperbole, litotes, meiosis, metonymy, oxymoron, paradox, paralipsis, paronomasia, periphrasis, personification, prosopopoeia, rhetorical question, syllepsis,

synecdoche, and zeugma. Corbett and Connors, *Classical Rhetoric*, Chapter Four.

15. W. Safire, *Lend Me Your Ears: Great Speeches in History* (New York: Norton, 1992), p. 664.

16. These four questions developed from my work with a remarkable group of researchers into high-tech developments, alas now disbanded. With many thanks to the brilliant minds at Research Services.

17. A. H. Maslow, *Toward a Psychology of Being*, 3rd ed. (Hoboken, N.J.: Wiley, 1998).

18. Transparency is a relatively new concept that has been widely discussed. The formulation here is mine.

CHAPTER THIRTEEN

1. A. Mehrabian, *Silent Messages: Implicit Communication of Emotions and Attitudes*, 2nd ed. (Florence, Ky.: Wadsworth, 1981), Chapter Five.

2. Mehrabian, *Silent Messages*, Chapter Nine.

3. Persuasion is at the heart of the connection between the verbal and the nonverbal; this is my formulation.

4. That decision making is emotional is widely discussed; see, for example, T. Lewis, F. Amini, and R. Lannon, *A General Theory of Love* (New York: Random House, 2000), especially Chapters Three and Four.

5. Again, see Lewis, Amini, and Lannon, *A General Theory of Love*, especially Chapter Two.

6. A good example of this is D. Morris, *People Watching: The Desmond Morris Guide to Body Language* (New York: Vintage, 2002).

7. I was inspired by Susan Goldin-Meadow's research as reported in *Hearing Gesture: How Our Hands Help Us Think* (Cambridge, Mass.: Harvard University Press, 2003), especially Chapter Two.

CHAPTER FOURTEEN

1. The idea that you can influence your unconscious perceptions with conscious work seems to have begun with Soviet athletes training for the Olympics. A good formulation of it can be found in L. Bassham, *With Winning in Mind* (N.p., 1995).

2. The research was quoted in R. Conniff, *The Natural History of the Rich: A Field Guide* (New York: Norton, 2002).

3. S. Goldin-Meadow, *Hearing Gesture: How Our Hands Help Us Think* (Cambridge, Mass.: Harvard University Press, 2003), Chapter Three.

4. Goldin-Meadow, *Hearing Gesture*, Chapter Two.

5. D. Morris, *People Watching: The Desmond Morris Guide to Body Language* (New York: Vintage, 2002), especially pp. 71ff.

6. Goldin-Meadow, *Hearing Gesture*, Chapter Four.

7. Goldin-Meadow, *Hearing Gesture*, Chapter Two.

8. J. Tierney, "A World of Eloquence in an Upturned Palm," *New York Times*, Aug. 28, 2007.

9. See, for example, the chapters on the war years in M. Gilbert, *Churchill: A Life* (New York: Holt, 1991).

Acknowledgments

In the five years since *Working the Room* was published, I have had extraordinary opportunities to practice the theory expressed in that book around the world and with many wonderful clients. In the course of this work, I developed the ideas and approaches to communications explored in this book. I could not have either developed or practiced the ideas without the help of those clients, and to them I offer thanks and gratitude for their willingness to try, to learn, and to feed back.

Three clients in particular offered help with the manuscript of this new book; to them goes all the gratitude for the assistance and none of the blame for any errors here. Thanks to Tim Sanders, Alex Kinnier, and Jeff Johnson. All are wonderful speakers as well; catch them if you can. Jeff also contributed ideas in the section on the ancient Greeks, a subject about which he's both knowledgeable and passionate. Thanks for that too, Jeff.

Thanks are due to my agent, Jim Levine, for patiently working with me as the ideas evolved and the proposals proliferated. And thanks to Susan Williams at Jossey-Bass for being the wise one who saw the promise and got the point at a convention in the depths of winter in Chicago.

Thanks are due to Emma, Dave, Sarah, Eric, Thea, Howard, and Rita for patiently listening and vigorously commenting on these ideas as they have evolved. Thanks for speaking with the freedom and the love of an amazing family that spans two continents.

Finally, and most of all, there aren't thanks enough to give to Nikki, my partner, my fellow practitioner, my wife, and my soulmate, who heard these ideas first and has argued, cajoled, supported, refined, pushed, shaped, and carried me and these ideas from first mutterings to full realization in these pages. With her, everything is possible.

The Author

$\mathbf{N}$ick Morgan is one of America's top communication theorists and coaches. A passionate teacher, he is committed to helping people find clarity in their thinking and ideas, and then delivering them with panache. He has been commissioned by Fortune 50 companies to write for many CEOs and presidents. He has coached people to give congressional testimony, appear on the *Today Show*, and take on the investment community. He has worked widely with political and educational leaders. And he has helped design conferences and prepare keynote speeches around the world.

Morgan's methods, well known for challenging conventional thinking, have been published worldwide. His acclaimed book on public speaking, *Working the Room: How to Move People to Action Through Audience-Centered Speaking*, was published in 2003 and reprinted in paperback in 2005 as *Give Your Speech, Change the World: How to Move Your Audience to Action*. He has contributed to more than a dozen books and has coauthored several others.

He served as editor of the *Harvard Management Communication Letter* from 1998 to 2003. He has written hundreds of articles for local and national publications. He is a former Fellow at the Center for Public Leadership at Harvard's Kennedy School of Government.

After earning his Ph.D. in literature and rhetoric, Morgan spent a number of years teaching Shakespeare and public speaking at the University of Virginia, Lehigh University, and Princeton University. He started writing speeches for Virginia governor Charles S. Robb and went on to found his own communications consulting organization, Public Words, in 1997.

He can be reached at www.publicwords.com.

Index